Building Your Instructional Leadership

Building Relationships
Fostering Instructional Expertise
Navigating Complexities

Fran Prolman

THE
LEARNING
COLLABORATIVE

Published by The Learning Collaborative
Great Falls, Virginia
www.thelearningcollaborative.com

Copyright© 2017 by Fran Prolman

All rights reserved. No part of this book may be reproduced in any form or by any means, electronic or mechanical, including photocopying, recording, or by any information storage and retrieval system, without permission in writing by the author.

2nd edition, printed in Croatia, March 2017.

Distributed in the United States by The Learning Collaborative. Great Falls, Virginia.
Distributed in Europe by NSM Unlimited, Zagreb, Croatia.

The Library of Congress Cataloging-in-Publication Data
Prolman, Fran.
Building Your Instructional Leadership
Building Relationships, Expanding Your Instructional Toolkit, Navigating Through Complexities / Fran Prolman; foreword by Heidi Hayes Jacobs
ISBN: 978-0-9977553-0-5
1. Education 2. Leadership

*To my children,
Samantha and Gabriel.
You are my light, my heart and my hope for the future.
I love you forever and am so proud to be your mom.*

FOREWORD

Engaged professionals create possibilities for learners to soar. Why is it that some schools create those possibilities with regularity and vibrancy? It does not take long when roaming the halls and classrooms of a setting to literally see evidence of quality engagement between teachers and learners and colleagues and leaders. Despite all of the pressures, challenges, and tensions that do affect modern educators, there are determined professional teams that do make a difference and function effectively and collaboratively for the children in their care. In truth, the demographics or abundance of resources does not seem to be the key. Naturally, questions emerge: What makes the difference? How can we transform our school to be a creative and responsive place for growth? *Building Your Instructional Leadership* provides thoughtful answers, pragmatic directions, and human insights.

With characteristic intelligence and wit, Dr. Fran Prolman has taken the wealth of her experience working with schools throughout the world and has crafted a practical and moving guide. Having known Fran for over two decades and seen her in action, it is heartening to report on the enthusiastic response that teachers and administrators have when they encounter her teaching and coaching. Here is a sampling: "She makes so much sense. Our team is working with more openness and productivity". "I felt my perspective literally shift in working with colleagues". "She helps me laugh and take a breath. It all helps me to be more effective as a leader". Dr. Prolman is a seasoned professional with both organizational management skills and educational planning expertise.

What is impressive is that she integrates theoretical and pedagogical perspectives into her work and certainly does in this book. The reader will find thoughtful reasoning and psychological insight in her focus on what motivates educators to collaborate effectively, coupled with specific strategies to shape instruction and curriculum targeted to support student learning. It is a satisfying read, written with Fran's authentic voice and commitment.

What is more, the book is timely. We are well into the twenty-first century and there is palpable excitement about virtual learning, physical space design, modern curriculum and assessment design, and tech savvy students. Leaders need to be attuned to creating a culture of openness and optimism to shape contemporary environments. To be clear, this is not about the technology alone. Having one-to-one programs does not guarantee engagement. Relationships matter more now than ever in a school. Thus, Prolman's book provides needed guideposts to help leaders respond to our right-now learners.

Organized in three distinct yet mutually dependent sections, we explore how to develop personal leadership mindsets and skillsets adaptable to any learning setting whether a nursery school, elementary, secondary, college, or adult setting.

The first section, It's All About Relationships, gets to the heart of Prolman's approach She makes the case for creating a safe environment where all members of a school community can speak their truth and share their perspectives. Creating trust between professionals leads to trust with children and is foundational to learning. What is more, the author strikes a timely chord in cultivating empathy and appreciation for the common experience we have as human beings who happen to work together. The goal is lay the groundwork for supporting high functioning teams who can dedicate effort and energy to provide a meaningful and innovative education for learners.

The second section moves naturally to the Nuts and Bolts of Instructional Leadership. What I find impressive is that she has hit the refresh button on a range of topics needing updating and refurbishing: defining learning targets, crafting success criteria, and searching for evidence of learning in student products and performances. These critical topics have been examined for many years in the field, but not through the lens of relationship-based leadership. What is more, there are chapters detailing the importance of thoughtful learning observations, coaching conversations, and honest and descriptive feedback as central to helping students improve their own performance and gain confidence. In particular, Prolman connects the work in this practical second section directly with the first section of the book with her focus on cultivating "culturally proficient" instruction through defining what it looks like to be aware and sensitive to the culture of learners and the adults who work with them.

Rather than avoiding the real challenges that affect the health of a learning environment, Prolman takes them on directly in the third section of the book, Strategies for Confidence in Complex Situations. Given human nature in the close quarters of a school there will inevitably emerge tough encounters. Whether it is when faculty members bristle at "another new initiative" or there is toxic competition between teachers, leaders need skills to respond effectively. The people who work in a school have personal living conditions that might be problematic, and those troubles can make their way to a school. How does a leader assist without crossing a boundary? This section lays out steps and skills for having hard conversations, dealing with difficult people, working with resistance and confronting passive-aggressive behaviors not only with staff but with the community as well. Finding strategies to deal with the toughest moments in school life is critical for making the instructional possibilities and collaborative relationships operational. Pacing one's personal energy and stamina are central to leading and is rarely discussed in leadership conferences, but, in this last section Prolman does examine the issue and provides meaningful support and recommendations.

What I believe Fran Prolman is asking us as educators to do is expand our perception of what it is to lead. She is engaging us to consider a shift away from "managing" schools to recognizing the primacy of fostering relationships. When a learning environment has a collaborative and caring network between professionals, there is a safety net to catch both any student but also any adult in need of support. With a keen sense of trust, people are more willing to take risks, innovate, and find joy in the work. This attitude is contagious. As we all know, children can sense right away how the adults in a school perceive the culture.

In particular, there is a pragmatic "through-line" in the book, providing crystal clear steps to assist interactions, to organize faculty, to prioritize instruction, and to shape meaningful learning experiences.

Being responsive to contemporary learners requires shedding old habits and trying on new perspectives of leadership in a school, which is not easy work. Yet, it is necessary work, given the needs of contemporary learners. Fran Prolman makes it easier by encouraging us to take concrete steps with the heart and excitement to renew, refine, and perhaps even recreate ourselves as instructional leaders who soar.

Dr. Heidi Hayes Jacobs
Curriculum Designers
Rye, New York

CONTENTS

INTRODUCTION 13

SECTION 1: IT'S ALL ABOUT RELATIONSHIPS

Chapter 1	Building Psychological Safety... 19
Chapter 2	Cultivating Empathy... 31
Chapter 3	Facilitating Trust and Collaboration................................... 45
Chapter 4	Supporting High-Functioning Teams................................. 57

SECTION 2: EXPLORING THE NUTS & BOLTS OF INSTRUCTIONAL LEADERSHIP

Chapter 5	Learning Targets... 71
Chapter 6	Looking for Proof: Evidence of Student Learning.............. 83
Chapter 7	Giving Descriptive Feedback... 99
Chapter 8	Supporting Culturally Proficient Instruction and Learning Environments.. 111
Chapter 9	Observing for Learning... 123
Chapter 10	Coaching Conversations.. 137
Chapter 11	Addressing Mediocre Teaching....................................... 149

SECTION 3: STRATEGIES FOR CONFIDENCE IN COMPLEX SITUATIONS

Chapter 12	Navigating Through Change.. 169
Chapter 13	Building Your Conference Skill Repertoire...................... 181
Chapter 14	Dealing with Difficult People, Situations, and Conversations....... 193
Chapter 15	Building Your Own Resilience.. 203

APPENDIX 214

ACKNOWLEDGMENTS 220

ABOUT THE AUTHOR 222

INTRODUCTION

For years, I have known that our work in people-based organizations like schools is above all about relationships. Relationships are the currency that provides the greatest organizational power, and yet they receive the least attention. The main reason why anyone would do anything for anyone else is directly related to the strength of their relationship. Relationship building is like putting money into a bank. With every act of respect, appreciation, conversation, sincere interest, and empathic interchange, relationship deposits grow stronger. And yet, what I see from all of my practical work with schools, school systems, and review of the literature is that very little attention is given to leaders being intentional, conscious relationship builders first and foremost. *Building Your Instructional Leadership* seeks to address that gap.

In addition, the leadership identity paradigm in schools and school systems has shifted from an industrial age "building manager" to an intentional "instructional leader". However, when has that specifically been defined and supported? What are the actual skill sets, tools, and areas of emphasis which an instructional leader needs to have at the tip of their tongue with every observation, walkthrough, and conversation? *Building Your Instructional Leadership* addresses that need as well.

Lastly, relationship building and instructional leadership skills can all blow up in a minute if there is not an anticipatory set analyzing the context, the subtext, and the complexities of human beings as all of these skills are being implemented.

Building Your Instructional Leadership speaks to those situational complexities as well. *Building Your Instructional Leadership* highlights the relations between three skill sets: relationship building, instructional expertise, and navigating through complexities.

Section 1: It's All About Relationships will help leaders lay the foundation for instructional leadership. I refer to the relationship you have with yourself as a leader, the relationships you foster between the members of your team, and the ones you establish with every adult group with whom you work. The groundwork for these relationships begins with building an environment of psychological safety. A safe environment invites you to reflect on how you build relationships through intentional empathy, how you model and facilitate an environment of trust for all of those around you, and how you create and support structures for collaboration through your school. Building trust among adults, creating a psychologically safe environment to learn and grow together, and skills for collaboration and team building are the focus of this section. Every chapter ends with practical strategies and applications for you to experiment with as you and your faculty expand your relationship-building skillset.

Section 2: Exploring the Nuts & Bolts of Instructional Leadership will help leaders build a common language of expert instruction that correlates with student achievement. This section provides strategies for clarifying learning targets and the criteria for success which support them. It tells you how to look for evidence of student learning and proposes protocols for formative assessment of the collected evidence. This section also discusses the skills and tools for providing descriptive feedback aligned to the learning targets. It then moves on to culturally relevant instructional strategies and indicators of a culturally safe environment.

Section 2 also discusses the observational side of instruction such as the skills of observing classroom instruction and obtaining data-driven feedback. Through a variety of case studies you will also learn how to define and address mediocre teaching, what skillset is needed to coach conversations and how to design support structures to foster professional growth. As in Section 1, every chapter ends with practical strategies and applications to support your instructional skillset.

Section 3: Strategies for Confidence in Complex Situations is about strengthening your leadership when you are really tested. Anticipate "initiative fatigue" and faculty boycotting change; plan for difficult personalities adding toxin to the school atmosphere, and find out how to preserve a healthy environment. Learn how to refuel your own resiliency when you are being tested to the core.

This section will raise your level of consciousness and increase your disposition for strategic thinking and anticipation. It will highlight the skillsets necessary to address the complexities that instructional leaders deal with when facilitating professional growth for adults. It includes steps and skills for having hard conversations, dealing with difficult people, and working with resistance and passive-aggressive behaviors. As in the first two sections, every chapter in Section 3 ends with practical strategies and applications to help you navigate through the situational complexities of instructional leadership.

SECTION 1

Building Psychological Safety

HOW TO BUILD A PSYCHOLOGICALLY SAFE ENVIRONMENT

MANAGING THE POLARITY OF THE NEED FOR ACCOUNTABILITY AND THE IMPORTANCE OF PSYCHOLOGICAL SAFETY

> *"To create a psychologically safe environment requires at a minimum that you establish trust, boundaries, and a sense of control in the team or social environment."*
>
> Robert J. Marshak (2006)

According to the Harvard business professor Amy Edmondson, "Psychological safety describes the individuals' perceptions about the consequences of interpersonal risk in their work environment. It consists of taken-for-granted beliefs about how others will respond when one puts oneself on the line, such as by asking a question, seeking feedback, reporting a mistake, or proposing a new idea. One weighs each potential action against particular interpersonal climate, as in, 'If I do this here, will I be hurt, embarrassed or criticized?' An action that might be unthinkable in one work group can be readily taken in another, due to different beliefs about probable interpersonal consequences. " (Edmondson, 2008)

We know that psychological safety is a necessity in a thriving, inviting, and productive workplace. However, few people want to look incompetent, intrusive, ignorant, or negative in front of their colleagues or someone who evaluates them. Therein lies the dilemma. To build a psychologically safe environment means we seek to make mistakes and risk looking stupid, being seen as incompetent, or being labeled as a naysayer. It means that voice is sought and valued. That is where leadership skill becomes a necessity when building a psychologically safe environment (Edmondson, 2003). "In a healthy culture, nobody talks about screwing up or making a mistake because when you try new things the way people do in healthy organizations, people make mistakes all the time." (Ryan, 2016)

We also know the damage that comes from a psychologically unsafe working environment. Colleagues will no longer offer ideas. Faculty will spend their time protecting themselves, and might even get bonus points for throwing someone else under the bus. Every time a colleague withholds their thinking we rob ourselves and our colleagues of a learning opportunity. We shut down opportunities for innovation, creative energy, and synergy between us. We perpetuate a silo mentality and an industrial-age way of interacting that could be called "dog eat dog". It subverts collaboration and teamwork, which directly correlate with student achievement.

In addition to cognitive and collaborative shutdown, a very real physical phenomenon occurs when our sympathetic nervous system kicks in and hormones respond in turn to protect us. The "flight or fight" is a stress response triggered by fear or danger. Chronic activation of this survival mechanism is hazardous to your health. The "flight or fight" response makes your heart beat faster, your muscles tense up, and your breathing quickens. This can happen when you are in a traffic jam or a family argument. It can also happen when you are "called to the principal's office", being humiliated by a colleague in a department meeting, or being given a number on an evaluation rubric without any data behind it or support offered for you to evolve in your craft. For two years in a row, the American Psychological Association's annual stress survey shows that 75% of all Americans chronically experience moderate to severe stress. Given that most of our awake hours are spent on the job, this has huge implications for the environment in which we work and for the leaders to whom we report (Harvard Health Publications, 2016).

The World Health Organization states that depression, stress, and fatigue are ever present in the work force. Furthermore, they predict that depression will become the second most debilitating condition on the planet by the year 2020 (WHO, 2001).

How depressing is that? These are all the secondary effects of the flight or fight response that has become a constant in human physiology. Adults under chronic stress often seek help in the form of therapy, medication, or relaxation techniques such as yoga, meditation, or group support. This points to the necessity of studying and embracing the skills to build and support a psychologically safe environment (Harvard Health Publications, 2016).

When Dr. Edmondson conducted her groundbreaking research on effective organizations in hospitals and businesses throughout the United States (Edmondson, 2003), her findings were counterintuitive and inverse to her hypothesis. Teams and hospitals that made the most mistakes compared to any of their counterparts showed significantly higher success. The difference was what they did with their mistakes. They had a consistent infrastructure to study them, draw conclusions, and quickly implement lessons learned. Reflective practice was structured and expected. Dr. Edmondson has found that better teams are more willing to make and then discuss mistakes to get to the bottom of them. That can only happen in a climate of openness and psychological safety.

Imagine if the school environment also became the psychological safe haven we yearn for. Imagine a school community where it is expected to voice your concerns, questions, and ideas. Imagine when our learning becomes endless because the study of our mistakes is endless. We get to embrace our fallibility, our intellectual humility, and the blessing of learning together and supporting each other in a true learning environment.

HOW TO BUILD A PSYCHOLOGICALLY SAFE ENVIRONMENT

Building a psychologically safe environment means that all challenges and frustrations are reframed as a learning problem, approached in a spirit of inquiry. Some of the questions we might address in school include "How can we best foster learning given the existing obstacles?", "How can we be respectful when we have different viewpoints and belief systems?", "How can we invest in each other's professional growth?" Schools and the learning variables that they present entail enormous uncertainty. This is a great equalizer for every teacher. Uncertainty going hand in hand with faculty interdependence lessens the feelings of being overwhelmed, isolated, and hopeless. We are all here to learn from each other, support each other's growth, and help to think through the learning challenges our students raise. Uncertainty and interdependence invite everyone's voice, which, in turn, fosters psychological safety.

Psychological safety is also fostered when a leader courageously and openly models fallibility. We all bring our best selves to the table and we could all be missing something as we think through a problem. Brené Brown's research on vulnerability and the power of imperfection proves that strong leadership embraces our own imperfections as courage and strength. She says: "Vulnerability sounds like truth and feels like courage. Truth and courage aren't always comfortable, but they are never weakness[1]." She also explains that vulnerability is the birthplace of innovation, creativity, and change.

Lastly, a psychologically safe environment is built on the consistent modeling of curiosity. Asking questions becomes the key to learning and growing. Questions become the key to building voice among the adults. Seeking answers to questions strengthens the environment to become a true learning organization.

Figure 1. Psychological fear and psychological safety

MANAGING THE POLARITY OF THE NEED FOR ACCOUNTABILITY AND THE IMPORTANCE OF PSYCHOLOGICAL SAFETY

Dr. Barry Johnson, the creator of the term "polarity management" (Johnson, 2014), could add the polarity of accountability/psychological safety to his list of organizational challenges. The goal behind successfully managing any polarity is to know that each pole is not a problem to be solved. Both poles must exist in a healthy organization. A successful leader knows how to acknowledge polarity and make the best of both poles while maintaining the balance between the two. If there is so much psychological safety that we stop studying results and reflecting on our success, the faculty could become lax and less motivated. If accountability prevails, the faculty may become fearful, overwhelmed, and paralyzed. The challenge and leadership talent is to find a balance between the two, a creative tension between accountability adrenaline and psychological comfort.

The bottom left quadrant in the grid below (see *Figure 2*) illustrates what happens to an organization if there is no psychological safety, no demands, and no one is held accountable. It becomes a breeding ground for apathy. People do not commit themselves to the organization and they check out mentally and/or physically.

---

[1] Cover quote on the website of Brené Brown: www.brenebrown.com

If we provide lots of psychological safety but never hold people accountable for their work, the environment becomes too comfortable. It minimizes motivation, reflection, and risk taking, as portrayed in the top left quadrant. The bottom right quadrant, in turn, illustrates the interplay between low psychological safety and high accountability. This is where people become paralyzed with anxiety and live their work days in fear. The perfect place for every leader to strive for is the top right quadrant, where there is the right balance between psychological safety and accountability. People feel supported, safe to question and take risks, but never lose sight of the expectations to which they are held accountable.

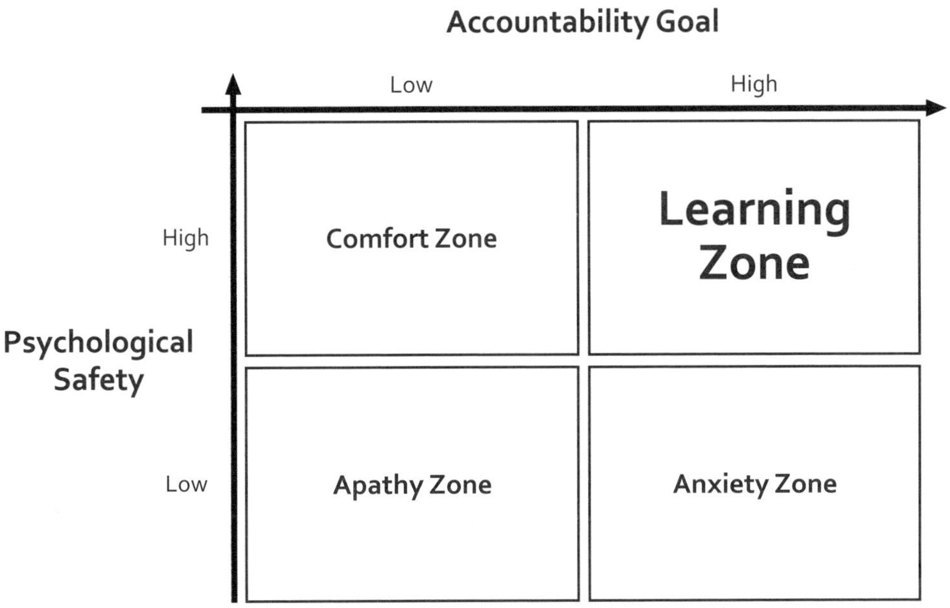

Accountability Goal

	Low	High
High (Psychological Safety)	Comfort Zone	Learning Zone
Low	Apathy Zone	Anxiety Zone

Figure 2. Psychological safety and accountability matrix[2]

Simon Sinek, an organizational researcher, designed a study chronicling the training process for soldiers seeking to become United States Marines (Sinek, 2014). He said that when the soldiers arrive they are insecure and lonely. They are put through a series of tests they are bound to fail if they try to solve them by themselves. Over time, they learn that their success depends on teamwork. They can only succeed in completing the tasks if they realize that they need each other, rely on each other, and help each other. When they eventually become marines and find themselves in harm's way, they rescue each other. They do not need medals or any other extrinsic motivator to want to do that. Their response is consistently "they would have done it for me". This idea that we are there for each other, the "circle of safety", as Simon

Sinek calls it, is directly determined by the quality of leadership. Leadership that does not foster instability and fear but rather builds individual and team capacity and does so in an environment of psychological safety.[3]

---

[2] adapted from Edmondson (2008)
[3] see Sinek's TEDTalk of March 19, 2014: "Why Leaders Make You Feel Safe" at www.youtube.com/watch?v=lmyZMtPVodo

Building Your Instructional Leadership

President Theodore Roosevelt has perhaps best formulated the psychologically safe environment and the importance of a leader who cultivates it:

> *It is not the critic who counts; not the man who points out how the strong man stumbles, or where the doer of deeds could have done them better. The credit belongs to the man who is actually in the arena, whose face is marred by dust and sweat and blood; who strives valiantly; who errs, who comes short again and again, because there is no effort without error and shortcoming; but who does actually strive to do the deeds; who knows great enthusiasms, the great devotions; who spends himself in a worthy cause; who at the best knows in the end the triumph of high achievement, and who at the worst, if he fails, at least fails while daring greatly, so that his place shall never be with those cold and timid souls who neither know victory nor defeat.*[4]

---

[4] Roosevelt, T. "The Man in the Arena", excerpt from the speech "Citizenship in a Republic" delivered at the Sorbonne, Paris, France on April 23, 1910. Available at: http://www.theodore-roosevelt.com/trsorbonnespeech.html

WHAT THIS LOOKS LIKE IN YOUR SCHOOL

A school leader who intentionally builds psychological safety, follows these steps:

1. Start with raising your own consciousness of the importance of psychological safety and become intentional about it. Raise your consciousness for opportunities to promote it, and nurture your disposition for it.

2. Trade in superficial "icebreakers" for purposeful activities of inclusion. To help the faculty learn who they are in relation to the group as a whole make meaningful connections with each other so they do not feel alone and realize and embrace faults as an indicator of a risk-taking, learning organization. Try some of the strategies in the Strategies section of this chapter.

3. Invite teams to study *Norms of Collaboration* (Garmston & Wellman, 2013) and reflect on how well they are being supported (for strategies see Chapter 3).

4. Look for opportunities to model your metacognitive process when you wonder and worry about issues as a leader. Think about how you solicit help and thought in partners and encourage your teacher leaders and faculty to do the same with each other.

5. Share the expectations you have of yourself and your faculty in terms of taking intellectual risks and reflections on the risks taken and lessons learned.

6. Honor strategic and professional mistakes you and/or your faculty have taken and what you would do differently because of the lessons learned.

7. Value asking questions of each other from a spirit of inquiry instead of judgment or interrogation.

8. Trade in the "either-or" language, which sets up a right/wrong culture, for the "both-and" language, which fosters safe and respectful dialogue. The "both-and" language values different perspectives and expands psychological safety.

9. Replace saying "I disagree" with saying "I see it differently". These words encourage a psychologically safe environment, which embraces diverse thought.

10. Foster invitational language by reframing a different opinion by saying "Another way of looking at it is…". Responding with "But…" or "However…" invalidates the thought or feeling that was just shared, argues with it, and damages psychological safety and honest dialogue.

STRATEGIES TO TRY

BUILDING A CULTURE OF PSYCHOLOGICAL SAFETY: INCLUSION ACTIVITIES

- *What's in a name*: With a small group of colleagues, your team or department, discuss the history of your name and how your parents or guardians gave you your first and middle name. What is the historical, religious, and/or cultural meaning of your name? What do you think of your name? If you could have picked a name for yourself, what would it be?

- *First job*: To build a community, participants introduce themselves and share information about their first paying job in the round-robin fashion. When all of the participants have shared, each person is invited to ask anyone in the group a question.

- *Check-in*: To increase mindfulness and mental presence within the group, the upcoming or relevant topic is named on a power-point slide with the following sentence stems:
  - "I have been thinking about _____."
  - "I have been feeling _____, because _____."
  - "Even though _____ has been on my mind, I'm in. I'm ready to focus on today's discussion."

  Example: "I have been thinking about the soccer game that the team I am coaching is playing right after this meeting. I am a nervous wreck."

- *"I am from..."*: A poem template to complete where every sentence begins with "I am from..." and you respond to the sentence stem. Stems are as follows:
  - familiar items found in the house/apartment/place where you grew up
  - sights, sounds, smells from your neighborhood
  - names of foods and special dishes served at special gatherings
  - familiar family sayings
  - people and names of relatives to whom you are linked

  Each person reads their completed poem to each other in the group or department, so write things you are comfortable sharing. Here is my own example, for you to consider as you create your own:

  I am from school principals, teachers, overnight camp directors, and the power-of-people dynamics where no one is shy.

  I am from the school calendar that started in September, ended in June, and overnight camp every summer when I got to come alive and be my best self.

  I am from Philly cheese steaks and soft pretzels and a lousy "Yo Adrien" Rocky Balboa accent.

  I am from Bubba's stuffed cabbage and matzoh ball soup and kreplach.

  I am from family holiday dinners with extra tables added that snaked through the house.

> I am from a household that never slept, energy, phones ringing, food on top of food, people always stopping by, no boundaries when it came to relationship building and high expectations, equal parts intellectual stimulation and exhaustion.
>
> I am from "always hide money in your garment"; "it could always be worse", "I don't care what everyone else got... are you everyone else?"
>
> I am from Audrey and Bill, Bubba Lesse, and the roots of Zhitomer outside of Kiev.

- *Artifact bags*: Each member of the team is given a brown paper lunch bag and asked to return the next day with five items that fit in the bag. The artifacts should be representative of them or important events in their life. They should fit the brown bag, so no microwaves! Also avoid photographs or items which you would be immediately associated with. Each item is symbolic or representative of the five most important parts of your life. The next day, each team member plays "archeologist" as the contents of one bag at a time are revealed. After the group thoughts on each artifact are shared, the owner identifies themselves and shares the accurate story.

- *Uncommon commonalities*: Each team brainstorms and makes a list of ten things that everyone has in common, yet which have nothing to do with education, your school, or your city. The team is invited to come up with as risk-taking and creative a list as possible (We are all human is not a big stretch.). When each team has ten items, they share them with the entire large group.

- *The street where I live*: Each team member is invited to draw a map of the neighborhood in which they were raised and mark five significant events that occurred in that neighborhood on the map. The maps are shared in their small group, so mention that each participant should be comfortable with the events noted, as they will be shared.

- *That's me*: Stand up in a large group if each sentence stem is true for you. Look around and see who else is the same as you in response to that stem. Then sit and wait for the next stem. Examples can be demographics (e.g. number of years teaching), geographic origins, number of languages spoken, favorite types of food/hobbies/types of music, etc.

- *Three truths and a piece of fiction*: Participants receive an index card and are invited to write four statements about themselves. Three are true, however unlikely they may seem (e.g. "I was on television"), and one is false but seems true. Each participant then reads out their card, and the team has to guess which of the statements are true or false before the author verifies or disproves their guesses.

- *I'm in*: Before the team meeting starts, each participant shares one sentence (can be run-on, multi-clause) that captures how their day has been going up until the beginning of the meeting. They end the sentence by establishing eye-contact with everyone in the room, and placing their a palm down onto the table declaring "I'm in".

BIBLIOGRAPHY

Bolman, L. G., & Deal, T. E. (2013). *Reframing Organizations: Artistry, Choice, and Leadership. Reframing Organizations.* http://doi.org/10.1177/019263650008461216

Brown, B. (2010). *The Gifts of Imperfection: Let Go of Who You Think You're Supposed to Be and Embrace Who You Are.* Center City, MN: Hazelden.

Brown, B. (2012). *Daring Greatly: How the Courage to Be Vulnerable Transforms the Way We Live, Love, Parent, and Lead.* New York, NY: Avery.

Cohen, D., & Prusak, L. (2001). *In Good Company.* How social capital makes organizations work. Boston, MA: Harvard Business School Press.

Edmondson, A., & Moingeon, B. (1999). *Learning, Trust and Organizational Change: Contrasting Models of Intervention Research in Organizational Behavior.* In Easterby-Smith, M., Araujo, L., & Burgoyne, J. (Eds.). Organizational Learning and the Learning Organization. London: Sage Publications.

Edmondson, A. C. (2003). *Managing the Risk of Learning: Psychological Safety in Work Teams* (pp. 255–275). In West, M. A., Tjosvold D., & Smith, K. G. (Eds.). International Handbook of Organizational Teamwork and Cooperative Working. Chichester, UK: John Wiley & Sons Ltd. http://doi.org/10.1002/9780470696712.ch13

Edmondson, A. C. (2008). The competitive imperative of learning. *Harvard Business Review*, 86(7–8), 60–67.

Garmston, R., & Wellman, B. (2013). *The Adaptive School: A Sourcebook for Collaborative Groups* (2nd ed). Lanham, MD: Rowan & Littlefield Publishers.

Garvin, D. (2000). *Learning in Action. A guide to putting the learning organization to work*, Boston, MA: Harvard Business School Press.

Gilley, J. W., & Maybunich, A. (2000). *Beyond the Learning Organization. Creating a culture of continuous growth and development through state-of-the-art human resource practices.* Cambridge, MA: Perseus Books.

Hargreaves, A., & Fullan, M. (2012). *Professional Capital: Transforming Teaching in Every School.* New York, NY. Teachers College Press.

Harvard Health Publications. (2016). Harvard Health. Retrieved 1 August, 2016, from http://www.health.harvard.edu/staying-healthy/understanding-the-stressresponse

Maira, A., & Scott-Morgan, P. B. (1996). *The Accelerating Organization: Embracing the human face of change.* New York, NY. McGraw-Hill.

Johnson, B. (2014). *Polarity Management: Identifying and Managing Unsolvable Problems.* Amherst, MA: HRD Press.

Marquardt, M. J. (1996). *Building the Learning Organization.* New York, NY: McGraw-Hill.

Marshak, R. J. (2006). *Covert Processes at Work: Managing the Five Hidden Dimensions of Organizational Change.* San Francisco, CA: Berrett-Koehler Publishers.

Ryan, L. (2016). *Forbes*. Retrieved 1 August, 2016, from http://www.forbes.com/sites/lizryan/2015/11/26/six-signs-of-a-broken-corporate-culture/

Senge, P. M. (1990). *The Fifth Discipline*. The art and practice of the learning organization, London: Random House.

Senge, P. M., Kleiner, A., Roberts, C., Ross, R. B., & Smith, B. J. (1994). The Fifth Discipline Fieldbook. *The Fifth Discipline Fieldbook: Strategies and Tools for Building a Learning Organization*, 593. http://doi.org/10.1108/eb025496

Senge, P., Kleiner, A., Roberts, C., Ross, R., Roth, G., & Smith, B. (1999). *The Dance of Change: The Challenges of Sustaining Momentum in Learning Organizations*. New York, NY: Doubleday/Currency.

Senge, P., Cambron-McCabe, N. Lucas, T., Smith, B., Dutton, J., & Kleiner, A. (2000). *Schools That Learn. A Fifth Discipline Fieldbook for Educators, Parents, and Everyone Who Cares About*. New York, NY: Doubleday.

Sinek, S. (2014). *Leaders Eat Last: Why Some Teams Pull Together and Others Don't*. New York, NY: Penguin.

Watkins, K., & Marsick, V. (Eds.). (1993). *Sculpting the Learning Organization. Lessons in the Art and Science of Systematic Change*. San Francisco, CA: Jossey-Bass.

Wheatley, M. (2007). *Finding Our Way: Leadership in Uncertain Times*. San Francisco, CA: Berrett-Koehler.

Wheatley, M. (2009). *Leadership and the New Science: Discovering Order in a Chaotic World*. San Francisco, CA: Berrett-Koehler.

Wheatley, M. (2009). *Turning to One Another: Simple Conversations to Restore Hope in The Future*. San Francisco, CA: Berrett-Koehler.

World Health Organization. (2001). *Mental Health: A Call for Action by World Health Ministers*. Geneva: World Health Organization. Retrieved from http://www.who.int/entity/mental_health/media/en/249.pdf

Cultivating Empathy

WHY EMPATHY IS A NECESSITY

HOW EMPATHY BECOMES THE ANTIDOTE TO SILOS

FOUR QUALITIES OF EMPATHY

SKILLFUL LISTENING

FOUR NEGATIVE TENDENCIES

SKILLFUL PARAPHRASING

HUMANITY IN YOUR SCHOOL:
THE ONE-THIRD, ONE-THIRD, ONE-THIRD RULE

> *"I used to think the worst thing in life was to end up all alone. It's not. The worst thing in life is to end up with people that make you feel all alone."*
>
> Robin Williams[1]

---

1 from *World's Greatest Dad* (2009) with Robin Williams as character Lance Clayton (more about the film is available at: http://www.imdb.com/title/tt1262981/?ref_=ttqt_qt_tt

WHY EMPATHY IS A NECESSITY

Empathy is the foundation for successful conflict resolution, embracing differences, problem solving, conducting richer and deeper analysis, and communicating more effectively. Without exaggeration, it is the key to world peace! Empathy also influences a teacher's ability to teach, a student's ability to learn, and an administrator's ability to lead adults. As a result, empathy needs to be in the forefront of your mind with every conversation, anticipation, and strategic decision you make as an effective instructional leader.

Empathy is a discrete skill we are all born with. The question is how empathy is identified, modeled, and nurtured? In fact, empathy can be defined, highlighted, practiced, cultivated, and reflected upon. This chapter will invite you to consider developing an "empathy fitness plan" that supports the adults (and students) in your organization with the skills of perspective-taking, collaboration, teamwork skills, cultural competency, professional collegiality, effective communication, active listening, and paraphrasing (Tavangar, 2014).

There are many reasons why teaching and modeling empathy is critical. There has been a measurable shift toward self-centeredness in children. The use of laptop computers, iPhones, iPads, and videogames only adds to student disconnection. There is a 48% drop in empathic concern for others over the past three decades. Low empathy leads to increased bullying and cyber bullying behavior.[2]

HOW EMPATHY BECOMES THE ANTIDOTE TO SILOS

With the increased push for removing silos within schools around the world (silos in the form of departments, subject area groupings, grade level teams, elementary, middle, and high school configurations on separate campuses or areas of a building), the new infrastructure must be built on a firm foundation of empathy to gain any traction. Collaborative structures, culturally proficient classrooms, teams and departments working together in a functional way, supportive peer observation, instructional coaching, and collegial behavior among adults cannot be fostered without empathy.

Jeremy Rifkin, the author of *The Empathic Civilization* (Rifkin, 2009) distinguishes between emotional empathy and cognitive empathy. Emotional empathy refers to our biological capacity to literally feel what another is feeling (enabled by our mirror neurons). Cognitive empathy involves our ability to accurately understand and interpret another's thoughts and feelings. Emotional empathy strongly correlates with our emotional intelligence, and cognitive empathy is the way to see through multiple perspectives.

Arthur Costa and Bena Kallick, the editors and authors of a book series entitled *Habits of Mind* (Costa & Kallick, 2009), have identified sixteen dispositions which successful

---

[2] I recommend watching That's What I Am (2011) with Ed Harris (more about the film is available at: http://www.imdb.com/title/tt1606180/

people exhibit in all walks of life. One of them is empathy. They explain that empathy helps people to behave intelligently when confronted with problems. They say that when people are in the midst of a contradiction, experiencing difficulty, confusion, or uncertainty, it is the action of empathy that creates a more powerful and significant result.

According to Vicki Zakrzewski, education director at the Greater Good Science Center at UC Berkeley, "...there is a very strong relationship between social-emotional learning and cognitive development and performance [...] Children as young as 18 months exhibit compassion, empathy, altruism, so these characteristics are part of who we are. But, at the same time, these skills have to be cultivated, because the environment can inhibit their development."[3] In other words, empathy, like a physical muscle, is present — but to manifest itself, it must be exercised. Homa Tavangar sums it up nicely: "An empathic environment is a smarter environment".[4]

Empathy can be discussed in a variety of ways. The Ashoka Foundation calls it "social fitness" (Laouri, 2016). Daniel Goleman calls it "emotional intelligence" (Goleman, 2005). Famed psychologist and Cambridge professor Simon Baron-Cohen measures what he calls the "empathy quotient" (Baron-Cohen, 2011). Nobel prize Laureate and psychologist Daniel Kahneman, in his book Thinking, Fast and Slow calls it "perspective taking in everyday life" (Kahneman, 2011). Simply put, empathy is the ability to step into the shoes of another person. The intention in the interaction is to understand their feelings and perspectives and to use that understanding to guide our actions.

Brené Brown, best-selling author and noted psychologist, has made ground-breaking discoveries in the areas of the power of vulnerability, shame, and empathy. Her TED talk on vulnerability is one of the five most watched TED talks ever produced[5]. She speaks about four qualities of empathy.

FOUR QUALITIES OF EMPATHY

The first critical attribute of empathy is perspective-taking. "Walking in someone else's shoes" is a metaphor that has been around for a long time, but what it actually entails is a sophisticated metacognitive process. For one, it means being able to step out of our own ego to notice someone else's. It also means having a desire to seek to understand. It is supported by a set of inquiry skills. It requires curiosity as well as compassion. It assumes that you are interested in learning from someone else. All of these skills become the foundation for cultural proficiency and the intentional building of a culturally proficient classroom. These skills are the backbone of global mindedness and of raising children to be concerned and caring citizens of the international world. They also help dysfunctional teams to get along, and administrative teams to build trust with one another.

The second attribute of empathy is withholding judgment. If you thought all of the

---

[3] see Homa Tavangar's blog (Tavangar, 2014)
[4] ibid.
[5] available at: https://www.ted.com/talks/brene_brown_on_vulnerability?language=en

discrete skills mentioned above are a challenge, try withholding judgment when you are judgmental by nature. And yet, this is a critical step toward cultivating empathy. Judging what someone says or how they feel has no place in an empathic interchange. A skilled communicator who has judgmental tendencies will always have judgmental tendencies. hey never go away. The difference is that a skilled communicator knows how to identify judgmental thoughts, see them float through their mind like a stock exchange tickertape that continually runs, and has the wisdom to muzzle every one of those judgments. They are never verbalized. This takes self-knowing, discipline, and humility.

The third attribute is recognizing emotion in other people. To be able to do this, we need to be mindful and present in the moment, pay attention and make eye contact and not be so immersed in our own agenda that we fail to notice what the other person is communicating to us verbally or non-verbally. This may not seem terribly difficult to do, but consider the reality of a school administrator: you are heading down the hall to observe a classroom, and every few feet you are stopped by a different person with a different need or agenda. It is not easy to stay focused, in the moment, and to listen actively, but can become an intentional disposition for someone who is actively cultivating empathy.

The fourth and last attribute is feeling with people. On some level, this could be the most challenging attribute of all. To actually feel with people means that we have to be willing to be in a vulnerable place to want to feel with that person. It means sharing the journey, the burden, and the pain. Brené Brown calls this a "sacred space"[6]. It is your willingness to say that you know what it is like to be overwhelmed, afraid, hopeless, lost, heartbroken, and that you are not alone. If in fact you have no experience with any of these emotions, then her recommendation is to simply say "I don't know what to say, but I am so glad that you told me." A fix-it response, a sugarcoated act of sympathy can never make it better. Connection is what addresses the situation, and only connection makes it better. Connection only occurs through empathy.

Figure 1 highlights the importance of self-management, self-awareness, relationship building skills, responsible decision making, and social awareness for a healthy, safe, and positive learning environment. Social awareness means recognizing and teaching empathy and showing an understanding for others. Based on the work of the Collaborative for Academic, Social and Emotional Learning (CASEL), this framework provides great support for school leaders, mentors, teachers, students, and their families.[6]

---

[6] Figure 1 was developed by the New Teacher Center and Acknowledge Alliance based on the work of the Collaborative for Academic, Social and Emotional Learning (CASEL) in 2013.

Figure 1. Social and emotional learning framework
(source: New Teacher Center and Acknowledge Alliance, 2013).

SKILLFUL LISTENING

Empathy sits on the bedrock of skillful listening. The term "paraphrasing" has been around for decades, so one might wonder haven't we figured out how to listen yet? As early as 1985, Arthur Costa and Robert Garmston suggested listening strategies in their text *Cognitive Coaching* (3rd edition, 2015), Bruce Wellman and Bob Garmston introduced practical paraphrasing skills in *The Adaptive School: A Sourcebook for Developing Collaborative Groups* (3rd edition, 2016), and Laura Lipton and Bruce Wellman elaborated on their listening and coaching work in *Data-Driven Dialogue: A Facilitator's Guide to Collaborative Inquiry* (2004).

Clearly, these skills are not new. So why are we still struggling with internalizing this skillset? It actually is complicated. Paraphrasing has been mocked as comic "parrot-phrasing" more often than not. Consider this interchange:

"I feel frustrated"
"It sounds like you are feeling frustrated".

This is an example of inept "parrot-phrasing" that makes the speaker feel like slapping someone! The ultimate goal of skillful listening is to keep our egos in check and manage the mental disruptions that can destroy an active listening interchange. And this is a real challenge!

FOUR NEGATIVE TENDENCIES

There are four tendencies that always get in the way of skillful listening. We all have at least one of these tendencies. Some of us are especially gifted and embody two, three, or four egocentric approaches to listening (egocentric listening - sounds like an oxymoron, doesn't it?). Left unbridled, these tendencies will shut down all active listening and, as a result, all empathic interchange. They are as follows:

1. **Interrogating**: When someone just wants to be heard, receiving a barrage of questions shuts down the conversation, makes the speaker feel like being on thevwitness stand, and invites defensive behavior. It leaves no room for skillfulvlistening that would lead to empathy.

2. **Storytelling**: When you actively listen to a colleague, their concern reminds you of the one that you had twelve years ago. You then proceed to dive into the context, details, characters in the story, and the person wanting to be heard is now shut down, ignored and disinterested in your personal story which was not asked for.

3. **Advice giving**: When a person just wants to be heard, being "fixed" like a human problem waiting to be solved is rarely appreciated. Receiving advice that was never asked for can be received as an insult, a condescending and patronizing interchange, and certainly does not foster empathy.

4. **Judging**: So many of us enjoy passing judgments in as many situations as possible. When a person wants to be heard, being judged fosters a sense of inadequacy, self-doubt, sorrow, and foolishness for starting the conversation to begin with.

If we are serious about building a culture of psychological safety, empathy, collaboration, and support, these four tendencies need to be explored, discussed, and grappled with on a daily basis. They never go away. We learn to know ourselves better and what it takes to manage our tendencies.

SKILLFUL PARAPHRASING

The Thinking Collaborative and their work in Cognitive Coaching provides three categories of paraphrasing skill to practice.[7] They all support the overall goal of cultivating empathy. The first category of paraphrasing is called "acknowledging and clarifying". Your responses for this context might include:

> You're thinking that...
> So, you're wondering if...
> You're frustrated because...
> You're hoping that...
> You're concerned about...

The second category, a match for people who might have many issues jumbled into one, who are circular in their thinking or lacking clarity, is called "summarize and

---

[7] visit www.thethinkingcollaborative.com for seminars based on Costa & Garmston (2015).

organize". Your responses to help someone summarize and organize their thinking might include:

> So, there are three issues...
> So, you have closure on ____ and you're ready to move on to ____.
> First you're going to ____, then you will ____.
> On one hand... and on the other hand...

The third category, which is the most sophisticated and requires the the deepest listening and interpreting is called "shift level of abstraction". It requires listening for what is actually never said. You need to listen for the subtext, for the submerged part of the iceberg. Examples of shifting up focus on listening for the underlying values, beliefs, goals, and concepts include:

> So, it's important to you that...
> So, a belief you hold is...
> So, you're a person who...
> A goal for you is...
> So, you're struggling with differentiation.

Shifting down means listening and paraphrasing through concrete examples. For instance:

> So an example of what you're talking about is...
> So this is not about...

Any of these categories and any of these stems let the speaker know that you are listening, seeking to understand, and checking if you are interpreting correctly.

HUMANITY IN YOUR SCHOOL: THE ONE-THIRD, ONE-THIRD, ONE-THIRD RULE

Some really lousy things can happen to us as we live our lives. These events and challenges are brought into your school every day. For instance, members of your faculty are currently struggling with children who are abusing substances and defying rehabilitation, grappling with serious psychological issues, or have been taken from this world all too soon. Or some of your faculty staff are nursing their parents or siblings through a terminal disease. Some of your colleagues are grappling with tragic events outside the school, which affect their livelihood and family structure. Our schools are microcosms of the world, and these scenarios of courageous educators reframing their lives around disease, loss, and frightening turns for the worse, play out in our schools every day. One third of every faculty is in this situation at any given time, trying to find the courage to get out of bed every day, to make eye contact with others, and to function. You may never know how much courage it took for someone to show up. The gift you give is your empathy.

The second third of your faculty are people who have been experienced the scenarios listed above but have portaged their way to the other side. The pain is recent enough, close enough, so they are humbled. They bring that raw piece of themselves to the faculty lounge and department meeting every day. They look through the lenses of humility, spirituality, vulnerability, and wisdom.

The last third of your faculty falls into the category that the Indian subcontinent calls "maya" or "illusion". The concept of illusion is something that you strive to rise above, to shed and no longer pretend to be in. Illusion is the belief that we actually have control; that we are on top of all things; that things happen to other people but not to us. One third of your faculty does not know what they do not know. They may not understand the pain that life can inflict or know how to show support. They may unintentionally say something thoughtless or hurtful to a colleague, because of their limited experiences. They truly do not know any better.

Nietzsche said: "Whatever does not kill me makes me stronger". He should have added: "…and it makes me humbled, empathic, and caring.". We do not leave our humanity and our experiences at the door. They come with us into every classroom every day, hopefully with compassion and empathy.

Chapter 2 / Cultivating Empathy

WHAT THIS LOOKS LIKE IN YOUR SCHOOL

A school leader who intentionally models and expects empathic behavior between and among adults and students takes the following steps[8]

1. *Create the conditions in which empathy can thrive*: listening, withholding judgment, showing respect.
2. *Create a safe space*: A trust-based environment is the core to unlocking empathy
3. *Lead by example*: Consider what empathy looks like in your interactions and reflect on how you can invite that behavior among your colleagues.
4. *Develop emotional competency*: Understand and manage your own emotions in order to identify and interpret emotions in others.
5. *Provide role-playing opportunities*, so your faculty can practice empathic responses with each other.
6. *Provide a group reading on empathy and facilitate a conversation on its implications in your school.*
7. *Identify shared values and differences* within the faculty. Name and appreciate the differences.
8. *Stand up to disrespectful behavior* and discussion which shuts down empathic response.
9. Discuss steps and strategies to *build your empathy muscle* (see below).
10. *Highlight the importance of empathic responses* by posting visible quotes in your newsletter and on your school's website.

---

[8] available at: https://startempathy.org/resources/toolkit/

Building Your Instructional Leadership

STRATEGIES FOR BUILDING YOUR EMPATHY MUSCLE

1. Have your faculty or departments watch and discuss the animated three-minute video on empathy at: https://www.youtube.com/watch?v=1Evwgu369Jw Discuss what this looks and sounds like to the adults at your school.

2. For a deeper dive watch Brené Brown's speech at TEDTalks: "The Power of Vulnerability" (20min; http://www.ted.com/talks/brene_brown_on_vulnerability). Discuss the implications individually and as a faculty.

3. Have each team watch and discuss Brené Brown's "Boundaries, Empathy, and Compassion (53 min; www.youtube.com/watch?v=ecb6ExBaW8o). Discuss implications and next steps as a team.

4. Review the "social and emotional learning framework" developed by the New Teacher Center with your faculty or in teams (see Figure 1 above). Do a jigsaw cooperative learning activity to brainstorm strategies to support each of the five categories.

5. Create an "empathy charter": how do we want to feel in school, and what obligations do we need to have to one another as a community?

6. Model "collective problem solving" to embrace alternative points of view and solutions.

7. Play "Six Thinking Hats" from the work of Edward DeBono to embrace six modes of thought or ways to respond to a situation (see Figure 2 below to support this strategy).

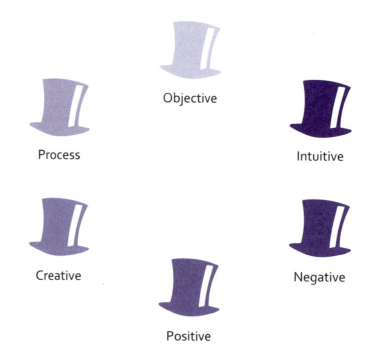

Figure 2. De Bono's Six Thinking Hats[9]

---

9   for more detail visit: http://www.debonogroup.com/six_thinking_hats.php

8. Plan a group read of the article, "The Dog's Wet and Life is Wonderful" by Donna Britt of *The Washington Post* (Britt, 1995). Discuss the role of gratitude that is modeled among us.

9. Review Maslow's hierarchy of needs and discuss how each of the following statements are supported by adults and with students in this community:

   - Autonomy: "I want to have a say in what happens to me."
   - Belonging: "I want to feel connected to and valued by those around me."
   - Competence: "I want to feel a sense of significance, worth and accomplishment."
   - Developmental Appropriateness: "I can only do what my brain and body are ready to do."
   - Engagement: "I want to have fun and be actively involved."

10. Design a personal coat of arms in response to six questions. A picture or a symbol goes in each of the six sections of the coat f arms. A template for this exercise is given below (*Figure 3*). Pick any six questions you are comfortable answering and sharing with your group:

    - What do you regard as your greatest personal achievement to date?
    - What is something about which you would never budge?
    - What is something you are striving to become or to be?
    - **What three things are you good at?**
    - **What is a personal motto you live by?**
    - What is one thing other people can do for yoxu to make you happy?
    - What do you like to do to make others happy?
    - If you could take one risk and you were guaranteed for success, what would that risk be?

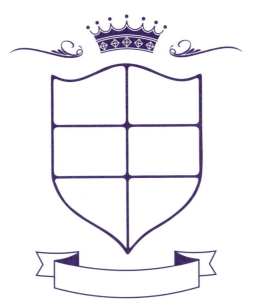

Figure 3. Template for your personal coat-of-arms[10]

---

[10] for more detail visit: http://www.debonogroup.com/six_thinking_hats.php

BIBLIOGRAPHY

Baron-Cohen, S. (2011). *The Science of Evil: On Empathy and The Origins of Human Cruelty*. Philadelphia, PA: Perseus Books.

Bedford, E. (2015, October 26). Activating Empathy to Fight Bullying in Schools. [Weblog]. Retrieved 2 August 2016, from https://startempathy.org/impact/article/activating-empathy-to-fight-bullying-in-schools/

Britt, D. (1995, June 16). The Dog's Wet And Life Is Wonderful. *The Washington Post*. Retrieved 2 August, 2016, from https://www.highbeam.com/doc/1P2-839676.html

Carr, N. (2011). *The Shallows: What The Internet Is Doing to Our Brains*. New York, NY: W.W. Norton and Company.

Costa, A., & Garmston, R. (2015). *Cognitive Coaching: Developing Self-Directed Learners and Leaders* (3rd ed.). London: Rowman and Littlefield.

Costa, A., & Kallick, B. (Eds.) (2009). *Learning and Leading with Habits of Mind: 16 Essential Characteristics for Success*. Alexandria, VA: Association for Supervision and Curriculum Development.

Durlak, J., & Domitrovich, C. (2015). *Handbook of Social and Emotional Learning: Research and Practice*. New York, NY: The Guilford Press.

Garmston, R., & Wellman, B. (2016) *The Adaptive School: A Sourcebook for Developing Collaborative Groups* (3rd ed.). London: Rowman and Littlefield.

Goleman, D. (2005). *Emotional Intelligence: Why It Can Matter More Than IQ*. New York, NY: Bantam Books.

Goleman, D. (2007). *Social Intelligence: The New Science of Human Relationships*. New York, NY: Bantam Books.

Kahneman, D. (2011). *Thinking, Fast and Slow*. New York, NY: Farrar, Strauss and Giroux.

Laouri, R. (2015, October 18). What our Brain Tells Us About Our Ability to Empathize. [Weblog]. Retrieved 2 August 2016, from https://startempathy.org/impact/ article/what-our-brain-tells-us/

Laouri, R. (2015, October 6). 5 Points for Your Empathy Arsenal: The arguments you need to explain why empathy is a key to life-long learning. [Weblog]. Retrieved 2 August 2016, from https://startempathy.org/impact/article/5pointsforyourempathyarsenal/

Rifkin, J. (2009). *The Empathic Civilization: The Race to Global Consciousness in a World in Crisis*. London: Penguin Books.

Tavangar, H. (2014, 7 August 2014). *Empathy: The Most Important Back-to-School Supply*. [Weblog]. Retrieved 2 August 2016, from http://www.edutopia.org/blog/empathy-back-to-school-supply-homa-tavangar

Wellman, B., & Lipton, L. (2004). *Data-Driven Dialogue: A Facilitator's Guide to Collaborative Inquiry*. Sherman, VT: MiraVia.

Facilitating Trust and Collaboration

BUILDING THE AFFECTIVE GLUE THAT HOLDS US TOGETHER
BUILDING TRUST INTENTIONALLY
THE POWER OF COLLABORATION
WHAT IS A COLLABORATIVE SCHOOL?
THE CHALLENGE OF COLLABORATION
PRINCIPALS NEED TO PROMOTE COLLABORATION IN THEIR SCHOOLS

> *"I've learned that people will forget what you said, people will forget what you did, but they will never forget how you made them feel."*
>
> Maya Angelou

BUILDING THE AFFECTIVE GLUE THAT HOLDS US TOGETHER

Trust cannot be taught. Trust cannot be built by asking people to fall out of trees so your colleagues can catch them or by asking colleagues to lead each other blindfolded through a forest, up and down stairs, or through a school building. If anything, these trite and superficial strategies can provide even more reason not to trust the leader, because they are silly and don't work. Instead, they suggest that your leader lacks competence to lead.

Leadership development author Simon Sinek describes both trust and loyalty as feelings.[1] You can't teach feelings. They are felt in response to events, behavior, and conversations. As a result, trust and loyalty have to be earned by the behavior modeled and conversations experienced with the leader. That takes behavioral consistency over time. A fair response to any leader asking you to trust them is "Why should I?" What is their track record of saying what they mean, meaning what they say, following through on promises made, and telling the truth? What is their track record of being transparent, seeking your input, and discussing how it was used or why it wasn't incorporated? It would be foolish to trust anyone and everyone without any data to support your choosing to do so. Equally, after extended time and evidence of trustworthiness collected, it would be like closing a door to opportunity if you never give your leader a chance. A leader saying "Trust me! Cooperate!" won't generate trust. It only comes from a leader who is intentional about building a psychologically safe environment (see Chapter 1) and who generates that trusting feeling. The trust evoked from modeling is obvious and consistent. It usually takes six to nine months for a trusting environment to be built. This environment nurtures and expands the feelings of trust among its inhabitants.

BUILDING TRUST INTENTIONALLY

Leaders need to take the intentional building of trust seriously to strengthen an environment of risk taking, mutual support, honest feedback, and continuous growth. Follow five entry points for leaders to intentionally build trust (Brafman & Brafman, 2010; Hammond, 2015).

1. **Modeling vulnerability**

    Leaders know that if they want their teachers to be honest with each other, willing to share their problems of practice and their mistakes and reflections about them, they have to model vulnerability first. A wise leader knows what boundaries to the vulnerabilities they share are appropriate. Brené Brown says that the ultimate act of bravery and courage (how we would characterize leadership) is sharing our vulnerabilities. The message is that we are secure enough with who we are to give up the pretense of perfection. We are always a work in progress.[2]

---

[1] See his TED talk at: http://ed.ted.com/on/AxQFPpJM
[2] Available at: https://www.ted.com/talks/brene_brown_on_vulnerability?language=en

2. **Cultivating familiarity**

   In addition, leaders know that psychological safety and trust are strengthened by familiarity. Familiarity in a school setting means that the leader is always popping in to each classroom asking how things are going and what additional support teachers might want; it means that the leaders are showing up at evening school events, supporting students' and teachers' school performances; that they are making themselves visible in the cafeteria and greeting everyone in the morning as the buses roll in or as the faculty check their mailboxes in the office. Familiarity does not breed contempt. Familiarity breeds a raised level of caring, of comfort, of paths crossing, of acknowledgment that we exist in the same sphere. That builds trust.

3. **Facilitating commonalities**

   Another way to build trust is to facilitate commonalities among the faculty. A leader heightens the awareness of our similar interests and hobbies. Who has children of similar ages? Who commutes the farthest to and from school? Which faculty members live near each other? Who went to the same university or have the same talents? Who are the great cooks in the faculty? The athletes? The second career switchers and what they did in their previous lives? Similarities build connection and connection builds trust.

4. **Inviting and acknowledging concerns and fears**

   The human condition includes all of us grappling with concerns and fears. They can be professional, personal, or both. A leader who models empathy, active listening, withholding judgment, and offering support is a leader who is also building an environment of trust. A leader who hears concerns or fears and helps them go away is a leader who knows how to build trust in a meaningful way.

5. **Proving competence**

   A leader who knows what they are doing, who brings a depth of background, confidence in decision making, a wealth of resources and support to draw from is a leader who models competence. A leader who knows the language of instructional pedagogy and provides descriptive data and feedback based on classroom observation builds confidence with the faculty as an instructional expert. A leader who coaches, leads faculty to solutions that work, helps others to expand their capacity — this leader shows proof of their competence. Competence enables teachers to feel confident in their leader.

Trust becomes the foundation of functional teams (see Chapter 4) and defines the level of collaboration between adults. Leaders need to know how to promote and facilitate collaboration, because collaboration among adults directly correlates with student achievement (Little, 1990).

THE POWER OF COLLABORATION

Judith Warren Little, the recently retired Dean of the University of California Berkeley Graduate School of Education, known as the pioneer in collaboration research, sought to answer the following questions:

- How central or peripheral are teachers' relations with colleagues to their success and satisfaction with students, their engagement in their present work, and their commitment to a career in teaching?
- What is the contribution that teachers' collegial involvement makes to the quality of the work force and the productivity of schools? (Little, 1982)

She found that working together increases the prospects of mutual influence among teachers and intensifies the exploration of beliefs teachers hold and the sharing of knowledge about a subject and the students. Joint work — the heart of collaboration — becomes central to teacher success and satisfaction with students, to their engagement in current work and to the productivity of the school.

WHAT IS A COLLABORATIVE SCHOOL?

A collaborative school is the one in which administrators and teachers routinely work together to promote effective teaching and learning. It is characterized by what Little calls the "critical practices of adaptability":

1. "Teachers engage in frequent, continuous, and increasingly concrete and precise talk about teaching practices" (as opposed to simply gossiping about other teachers, administrators, and students).
2. "Teachers are frequently observed and provided with useful feedback about their teaching."
3. "Teachers plan, design, research, evaluate, and prepare teaching materials together."
4. "Teachers teach each other the practice of teaching." (Little, 1982)

Little's work has been substantiated with further studies proving the power of collaboration by many researchers over the years, such as Susan Rosenholtz (1991), Deborah Meier (1987), Anne Lieberman (1984), Rick DuFour (DuFour & Eaker, 1998), and Stuart Scott (Smith & Scott, 1990). Tracy Crow, the Director of Communications at Learning Forward completed the most recent study on the power of collaboration in schools in June 2015 (Crow, 2015). This quote of hers best summarizes why collaboration is so important:

> "The ultimate goal of collaborative learning is better teaching, better student learning, better results for every learner in schools. Excellent teams - supported by committed leaders and sustained resources — create a culture where every professional in the school is responsible for every student." (Crow, 2015)

As a result, all students learn.

Chapter 3 / Facilitating Trust and Collaboration

THE CHALLENGE OF COLLABORATION

Collaboration requires a significant cultural shift in schools. The reality of teachers working in isolation, of being organized into silos, and of the silo mentality that goes along with that can brew real resistance to the vision of collaborative interaction among the adults. This vision challenges entrepreneurial individuals whose autonomy is grounded in norms of privacy. The vison of collaboration goes head to head with an expectation of non-interference and being left alone. When pressed, it is possible to come to every collaborative interaction with a laissez-faire view of compliance without any of the commitment toward making collaborative relationships work.

PRINCIPALS NEED TO PROMOTE COLLABORATION IN THEIR SCHOOLS

Principals can promote collaboration by shifting the focus from their voice to the teachers'. Collaboration in school means involving faculty members in setting the agenda for faculty meetings, facilitating teacher analysis of student data, discussing instructional implications in response to data trends, and manipulating the master schedule so that teachers can plan together. Teachers trained to observe each other and address their problems of practice together also serve the goal of collaboration. Although formal structures and strategies can help to facilitate collaboration, collaboration ultimately depends on the development of a set of norms among the adults. Just because you create the time and the place, this doesn't ensure that adults actually know how to interact, listen respectfully, monitor their own behavior, and be aware of the behavior of their colleagues when put together to collaborate, especially where teachers have been isolated in their classrooms (Garmston & Wellman, 2009).

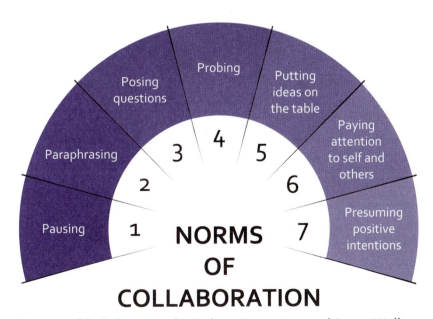

Figure 1. Norms of Collaboration by Robert Garmston and Bruce Wellman (2009)

Robert Garmston and Bruce Wellman developed seven norms of collaboration to support their research and work with schools adapting to new challenges. These seven norms can be taught, reflected upon, and practiced over time. They are essential to the effectiveness of group collaboration.

1. **Pausing**. This norm reminds colleagues to breathe, listen, and reflect on what is being said. It reminds people not to just wait until someone comes up for air to rush in with their own personal agenda, but rather to pause, wait, and show respect for what is being shared. It keeps colleagues from cutting people off and from talking over each other.

2. **Paraphrasing**. This norm provides the gift of not just being listened to and heard but actually being understood. Actual sentence stems for paraphrasing are shared in depth in Chapter 2 (Cultivating empathy). When a colleague paraphrases, they are not passing judgment of what they heard. They are only checking if they heard it correctly.

3. **Posing questions**. After a colleague has given the confirmation that they have indeed been heard correctly, it is appropriate to ask open-ended, non-accusatory questions in the spirit of inquiry and seeking to understand.

4. **Putting ideas on the table** invites brainstorming and fluency of thought. When ideas are put on the table, they are not judged. They are collected and might spur additional ideas playing off of each other. Actually discussing the ideas and rating them against criteria for a decision happens much later in the process.

5. **Providing data**. This refers to data that confirm or deny aspects of a conversation or provide additional information or a clarification. Providing data also reflects a wish to explore implications based on data analysis and what has been discussed. These data provide a "third point" — a neutral piece of information that does not judge or accuse — for colleagues to study. They provide objectivity and keep the conversation from getting personal. The focus is on the third point, which is the data.

6. **Paying attention to self and others**. This norm invites colleagues to take notice and raise their own emotional intelligence about their behavior and how it affects others in the group. Paying attention to self means listening to one's own choice of words and tone, noticing how others react to how you communicate, and noticing others in the group: their use of time, honoring the agenda, staying focused, and level of respect toward others.

7. **Presuming positive intentions**. This norm gives everyone the benefit of the doubt, and everyone is innocent unless proven guilty. This norm reminds all members of the group to withhold judgment and know that everyone is bringing their best self to the table at that moment.

In high-performing groups, these norms of collaboration become posters hanging in the room where meetings are held. They are tent cards on the conference table, and every member reviews them and holds themselves accountable to upholding them. They become the basis for reflection at the end of the meeting, so each member can think about how they contributed to the intellectual and emotional health of the team.

	Be Present and ABSORB
A	Attention
B	Body language and tone of voice
S	Stop and focus
O	Open to understanding, not judging
R	Repeat through paraphrase
B	Becalm the gremlins

Figure 2. ABSORB by Kathy Taberner and Kirsten Siggins
(adapted from Taberner & Siggins, 2015).

In addition to the norms of collaboration, Kathy Taberner and Kirsten Siggins (2015 offer an acronym to remind groups of similar skills to uphold mindfulness in the collaborative group. The ABSORB model is a gentle reminder to think about the kind of attention we give, our body language, which communicates louder than words, and the importance of monitoring our judgments that have no place in open, honest communication. The ultimate goal of collaboration and adults learning together is expanding student achievement. High-performance collaborative teams (See Chapter 4 for more information), supported by committed leaders, make this happen. A skilled instructional leader is a teacher of and a model for collaboration skills necessary for shifting the paradigm from "I" to "we".

WHAT THIS LOOKS LIKE IN YOUR SCHOOL

A school leader who intentionally models and expects trusting and collaborative behavior between and among adults and students models the following:

1. Making daily rounds in and out of classrooms to make eye contact with teachers and students and to collect good news that is going on in their lives and in their classrooms.
2. Seeking to find points of connection with teachers and for teachers to find them with each other.
3. Sharing areas of concern or fear and how they will be addressed.
4. Asking for help and expecting the faculty to do the same with each other.
5. Sharing resources to expand our professional craft.
6. Creating time for teachers to work collaboratively [see Valerie von Frank (2013) for ideas on how to do this].
7. Providing training in norms of collaboration, so that adults know how to interact skillfully with each other during collaborative time.
8. Honoring confidentiality at all times and making gossip an unacceptable norm of behavior.
9. Celebrating the successes of the faculty and students.
10. Speaking from a position of facts as opposed to judgment.

STRATEGIES TO TRY
BUILDING TRUST AND COLLABORATION

1. Manipulate the master schedule in a way that provides time for collaborative conversation;
2. Review the seven norms of collaboration and what they look and sound like with each team or department;
3. Role play how to paraphrase and actively listen to each other;
4. Practice using protocols together to examine student work (see the following pages about protocols to foster collaboration) and to discuss next instructional steps;
5. Facilitate teachers' collaborative planning based on the use of standards, learning targets, formative and summative assessments;
6. Watch teaching videos together and analyze the teaching strategies and their effect on student learning (use www.teachingchannel.com for thousands of free videos to choose from);
7. Engage in instructional rounds together, looking for patterns and trends of teaching and learning;
8. Adopt and practice collaboration models such as the use of data teams, looking at students' work together, peer observation, and planning lessons together;
9. Video record your own teaching and discuss lessons learned with a colleague; 10.
10. Bring up problems of practice to the group to assist each other in brainstorming potential solutions and providing problem-solving support.

BIBLIOGRAPHY

Brafman, O., & Brafman, R. (2010). *Click: The Forces Behind How We Fully Engage With People*, Work and Everything We Do. New York, NY: Random House.

Crow, T. (2015). Keys to Collaboration. JSD, 36(3), 10 – 12.

DuFour, R., & Eaker, R. (1998). *Professional Learning Communities at Work: Best Practices for Enhancing Student Achievement. Bloomington*, IN: Solution Tree Press.

Garmston, R., & Wellman, B. (2009). *The Adaptive School: A Sourcebook for Developing Collaborative Groups* (2nd ed). Norwood, MA: Christopher Gordon.

Garmston, R. (1997). Can Collaboration Be Taught? *Journal of Staff Development*, 18(4). Available at: http://myvolusiaschools.org/professional-learning/Documents/PLCs/CanCollaborationBeTaught.pdf

Hammond, Z. (2015). *Culturally Responsive Teaching and The Brain* (p. 79). Thousand Oaks, CA: Corwin Press.

Lieberman, A., & Miller, L. (1984). *Teachers, Their World, and Their Work: Implications for School Improvement*. Alexandria, VA: Association for Supervision and Curriculum Development.

Little, J. W. (1982). Norms of collegiality and experimentation: Workplace conditions of school success. *American Educational Research Journal*, 19(3), 325–340. http://doi.org/10.3102/00028312019003325

Little, J. W. (1987). Teachers as Colleagues. In Richardson-Koehler, V. (Ed), *Educators' Handbook: A Research Perspective*. New York, NY: Longman.

Meier, D. (1987). Success in East Harlem: How One Group of Teachers Built a School That Works. American Educator, 11(3), 34 – 39.

Rosenholtz, S. J. (1991). *Teachers' Workplace: A Study of Social Organizations*. New York, NY: Longman.

Smith, S. C., & Scott, J. J. (1990). *The Collaborative School: A Work Environment for Effective Instruction*. Eugene, OR: ERIC Clearinghouse on Educational Management and National Association of Secondary School Principals.

Taberner, K., & Siggins, K. (2015). *The Power of Curiosity: How to Have Real Conversations that Create Collaboration*, Innovation and Understanding. New York, NY: M and J Publishers.

Von Frank, V. (Ed.). (2013). *Establishing Time for Professional Learning*. Oxford, OH: Learning Forward.

Supporting High-Functioning Teams

WHY TEAMWORK MATTERS

TEAMS MATURE BY MOVING THROUGH PHASES

TEAMS IMPROVE BY DIAGNOSING AND ADDRESSING THEIR DYSFUNCTIONS

TEAMWORK CORRELATES WITH STUDENT ACHIEVEMENT

> *Teamwork is often like the weather — everyone talks about it, but often nobody does anything about it. It is seldom achieved by intellectualizing, but i rather the practical application of attitude, common goals, and experience working together. It is a learned art.*
>
> Twyman L. Towery (1995)

WHY TEAMWORK MATTERS

When teams don't work together and every dysfunction is on display, productivity, efficiency, morale, absenteeism rates, reputation, and success are all compromised (Senge, 2012). Teamwork is so critical to the success of any organization that you can easily find monthly articles of tips and advice for making teams work in business, education, and organizational development magazines[1]. Schools, hospitals, and businesses care deeply about the effectiveness of their teams, because their effectiveness directly correlates with the success of the organization (Edmondson, 2012). The work of Edmondson, Senge, and others can be applied to administrative and teacher teams in every school, to the administrative and leadership teams in the central office, and to the senior staff teams, which provide the vision and support for the superintendent. All of these teams have tremendous implications for the students, how they learn and achieve. Because teamwork directly correlates with school effectiveness, this chapter will highlight the attributes of effective teams and the obstacles that get in their way. It will discuss the strategies to ensure team cohesiveness and to support teams.

Four reasons why teamwork matters

Amrita Nandagopal, a prolific researcher of team effectiveness clearly states that there are four reasons as to why teams achieve higher results (Nandagopal, 2013).

> **Motivation grows.** One piece of proof is that team members get more motivated. There is a powerful connection between people who are working toward a common goal and who are in close contact with each other on a daily basis. This connection has the potential to create synergy, support, and loyalty. When voices are contributed and heard, the team becomes a psychologically safe and trusting haven and an exciting place for new ideas. The power of human innovation comes to the forefront. Daniel Pink discusses this dynamic of motivational process through teams in his groundbreaking book called Drive (Pink, 2011).
>
> **Efficiency improves.** There are many ways in which teams can heighten their efficiency. One way is by systematizing the use of group roles during every team meeting. When teams routinely have volunteers who take on and share the roles of the facilitator, time keeper, note taker, and agenda organizer, efficiency improves. Dividing tasks within the group to meet deadlines improves efficiency. When one person is absent, there is instant backup for what they were entrusted to do. When the team organizes the work to be done by everyone's strengths and interests, efficiency expands as well (Rath & Conchie, 2009).
>
> **Adult learning is accelerated.** We learn more through collaboration and collegiality (DuFour, 1998; Little, 1982). We learn less when we are organized and stay inside our silos. As a result, teamwork expands our intellectual capacity by brainstorming with each other and by sharing our perspectives, backgrounds, and experiences. Diverse opinions challenge viewpoints and possibilities within

---

[1] One such online magazine is The Marshall Memo, available at: http://www.marshallmemo.com/

teams.

Interpersonal skills increase. Effective teams learn to establish norms of respectful listening. The participants model the seven Norms of Collaboration (see Chapter 3) and constantly have their finger on the pulse of the emotional health of the group individually and collectively. Participants seek to invite all voices into the room. Team members learn to model respect for each other by withholding judgement and by staying focused on discussing the work and not each other. These emotional intelligence skills foster the feeling of connection between group members. As a result, hopes, fears, and concerns are all expected components of effective team conversation.

TEAMS MATURE BY MOVING THROUGH PHASES

Forming

In 1965, Bruce Tuckman proposed a developmental sequence for teams which still rings true today (Tuckman, 1965). He said that all teams begin by forming. The critical attribute in the forming phase is that everyone is polite and on good behavior. Polite conversation, staying away from anything controversial, and never saying what you really think are the critical attributes of the forming stage. The problem with some teams is that they stay in the forming stage for their entire time together. This means that the team is guaranteed to stay superficial, to never dig into the real work of an interdependent team, and to avoid conflict and real interchange at all costs.

Storming

Some teams are brave enough to move out of the forming stage into what Tuckman calls the storming stage. Storming is an unfortunate term, because a storm evokes a negative connotation. Storm clouds are dark and scary. They require us to hide from the elements, to batten down the hatches, to close the shutters, and nail wood over the windows because a raging storm can create damage. If we were to replace the term "storming" with "cognitive debate", we would better capture the essence of this second phase. In high-performing teams, storming or cognitive debate suggests that the team members are willing to be honest with each other, even if it means that they disagree. They do not shy away from conflict. They hopefully have the skills to navigate through conflict and alternative points of view with diplomacy and respect. Strong leaders and team members appreciate this phase. They are not afraid of being there, because they know that storming is the spark which promotes creativity and innovation.

Norming

When teams are brave enough to portage their way through storming rather than run away from it, they come up with a unified and interdependent new vision. They are then ready to design new norms of interacting with each other. They can design new norms for rolling out the new plan, new norms for roles each member plays, and new norms for future ventures.

Performing

The last phase which Tuckman describes is the performing phase. This phase is totally anticlimactic. All of the interpersonal interchange, navigation, and regrouping is completed. Now the team rolls out the product or production. The real work is done in the storming and norming stages. The forming and performing stages are the shallowest and safest psychologically. In highly impatient systems, where there is no time for process and real interchange, a team is often asked to move from forming to performing immediately, which guarantees a shallow product and no relationship depth between the team members. Emotion and interdependency come from leaders seeking to maximize storming and norming and minimizing forming and performing.

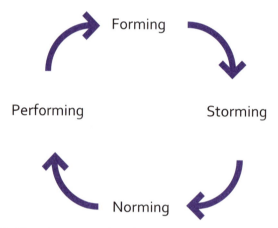

Figure 1. Stages of effective team development (adapted from Tuckman, 1965)

TEAMS IMPROVE BY DIAGNOSING AND ADDRESSING THEIR DYSFUNCTIONS

A psychologist colleague recently asked me where I have been spending most of my professional time. I told him it was with dysfunctional teams, and he laughed. "What team isn't dysfunctional?" he commented. He is right. There are so many sophisticated skills required of each team member in a high-functioning team. Unless each team member is serious about learning them, there will be some level of dysfunction. This reality is so prevalent that Patrick Lencioni wrote a bestselling book entitled *The Five Dysfunctions of Teams* (Lencioni, 2002). The five dysfunctions can be used by any leader as a diagnostic tool to analyze what is prohibiting each specific team from interacting at a high level. In Lencioni's model, the largest team problem is the lack of trust. Without trust no team member is willing to interact with each other. Trust is so important that it is part of a separate chapter in this book (Chapter 3), suggesting specific strategies to build it.

When a team is willing to be vulnerable, supportive, honest, and loyal to each other, real teamwork can begin, that is, until the next glitch. When real team interchange happens, there are bound to be disagreements and different points of view. Dysfunctional teams are afraid of conflict. They shy away from it because they don't have the skills to navigate through it. They move into Tuckman's forming stage, park there, and refuse to embrace his storming stage. This keeps the team in a superficial, nonproductive place. They have artificial harmony and a low level of productivity.

If a team is willing to participate in honest interchange, the next dysfunction roadblock is the lack of commitment. Commitment requires clarity of purpose, consistent understanding and interpretation of the team's goals, and a willingness to support them. Dysfunction rolls in when there is a lack of clarity and focus. Ambiguity clouds the path to team productiveness. Team members all have different interpretations of what needs to be done and thus go their different ways.

Dysfunctional teams are not interested in embracing individual and team accountability. Often team members blame each other or external variables for their lack of success. A way to avoid accountability is to lower the standards. There are low expectations, low standards, and low work output and quality.

Lastly, dysfunctional teams are not interested in their results. There is no curiosity to collect information on their success, to reflect on how they can improve, to discuss strategies for working together at a higher level. This kind of dysfunction manifests itself in ego and self-deception. Their perception is much more interesting than the results that reality may provide.

A skillful leader knows how to study teams to diagnose their dysfunctions and then seek to provide skills and support that directly correlate with the diagnosis. There are specific skills to build trust, to learn how to navigate through conflict (see the strategies page of this chapter), build commitment and accountability, and pay attention to results (Shmoker, 2006a; 2006b).

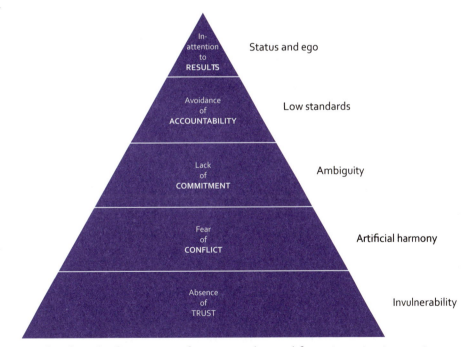

Figure 2. The five dysfunctions of teams (adapted from Lencioni, 2002)

Building Your Instructional Leadership

TEAMWORK CORRELATES WITH STUDENT ACHIEVEMENT

There is a direct correlation between adult interaction and student achievement (see Chapter 3). That being said, the term "teamwork" is a collage of each individual making his or her individual decisions and actions within the team. If the entire team, with the exception of one person, is all rowing in unison, but the lone team member is in the back of the boat successfully drilling a hole through the bottom so water flows in, the entire team will sink. Group behavior — how teams work together — is a picture of the decisions and actions of individuals and how they affect the team as a whole. Robert Garmston and Bruce Wellman suggest that when individual choices of behavior align with the goal of the group, the group functions well. When individual behaviors and decisions are at cross purposes, the group will be compromised (Garmston & Wellman, 2013).

This presents an opportunity for each leader to build capacity with each individual team member, so their contributions are aligned and helpful in achieving the group's goals.

Teams who are interested in raising their level of effectiveness embrace the uses of protocols like the Charrette or the Tuning Protocol designed by the National School Reform Faculty[2]. These protocols support the process of collaborative review and provide structure for offering suggestions on adult work.

A team might also discuss the behaviors and attitudes they bring to the team, as evidenced by the list below, created by a group of anonymous colleagues (*Figure 3*).

10 things that require zero talent
1. Being on time
2. Work Ethic
3. Effort
4. Body language
5. Energy
6. Attitude
7. Passion
8. Being Coachable
9. Doing Extra
10. Being Prepared

Figure 3. The list of behaviors and attitudes each member brings to the team

Roland Barth, Harvard professor and school practitioner, hits the nail on the head when he says:

> *Four years of school teaching — and ten years as a principal — convinces me the nature of relationships among adults who inhabit a school has more to do with a school's quality and character, with the accomplishments of its pupils and the professionalism of its teachers than any other factor.* (Barth, 2001)

---

[2] Both are available at: www.nsrfharmony.org

Chapter 4 / Supporting High-Functioning Teams

WHAT THIS LOOKS LIKE IN YOUR SCHOOL

1. Rearrange the master schedule to create time when teams can meet regularly.
2. Provide purpose, structures, and protocols to help the team focus on the work.
3. Offer opportunities for teams to reflect on their interactions and discuss ways to raise their efficiency and effectiveness.
4. Clarify roles within the team.
5. Support the freedom and empowerment of each team member to contribute and make decisions.
6. Build group member capabilities through the skills of discussion, withholding judgment, seeking to understand and decision making.
7. Discuss the cultural shift this team requires with each group member and why it is necessary for student achievement.
8. Expand capacity by studying how conflict can bring positive energy and creativity to the team.
9. Provide recognition and reward for team successes.
10. Encourage team risk-taking and experimentation.

Building Your Instructional Leadership

STRATEGIES TO TRY
BUILDING EFFECTIVE TEAMS

1. Have each team member take the Strength Finders quiz[3] and discuss what each team member offers (Rath & Conchie, 2009).

2. Read the article "Are You Using the Pinch Theory of Management" by Randy Clark (2011) and discuss and practice the language of how to address conflict between team members.

3. Study the four group member capabilities (Garmston & Wellman, 2013):
   - to know one's intentions and choose congruent behaviors;
   - to set aside unproductive patterns of listening, responding, and inquiring;
   - to know when to self-assert and when to integrate;
   - to know and support the group's purposes, topics, processes, and development

   Have the team read, study, discuss, and practice each of these behaviors and receive feedback on how they are being enacted.

4. Teach teams how to use creative problem solving to address challenges which come their way using the model created by Donald Treffinger. See his steps in *Figure* 4 below and test it against a problem of practice your team might be experiencing.

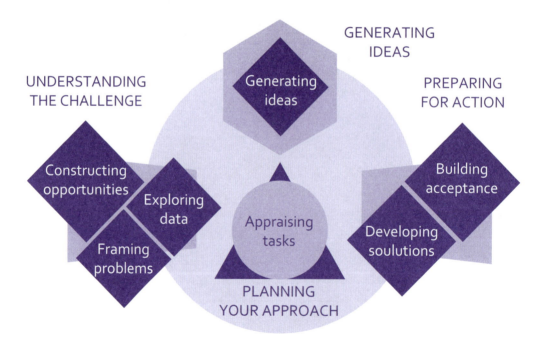

Figure 4. The creative problem-solving framework (adapted from the framework designed by the Creative Problem Solving Group, Inc.)[4]

---
3   available at: https://www.gallupstrengthscenter.com
4   available at: http://www.cpsb.com & http://www.creativelearning.com

5. Create a team charter to define each person's role, the projected team outcomes, and expectations each team member has for each other.

6. Design a team mission and vision statement.

7. Use the Betari Box below (*Figure 5*) to discuss the impact that our own attitudes and behaviors have on the attitudes and behaviors of the people around us.

Figure 5. How our attitude and behavior affect others

8. Have a conversation about the elephants in the room by asking "What conflicts within the team aren't we talking about?" and "How will we manage conflict now and in the future?"

9. Facilitate a conversation about conflict in the team. What are teammate belief systems about the role of conflict and how it is addressed and navigated. The true-or-false questions below might scaffold the dialogue.

Statement	True of False
1. Any disagreement between two people can be defined as a conflict.	
2. Conflict is a direct outcome of differences between people.	
3. Conflict can be perceived or actual.	
4. Disagreements are not welcome in teams.	
5. Conflict is normal.	
6. People can be involved in conflict without even knowing about it.	
7. Emotions have no role to play in conflict.	

(adapted from Manktelow & Brodbeck, 2009)

10. Create a pre-mortem; read "Performing a Project Premortem" by Gary Klein in the *Harvard Business Review* September 2007 issue (Klein, 2007). Have the team practice analyzing all of the potential concerns before they begin a project or initiative and list the concerns and possible solutions before they begin their work.

BIBLIOGRAPHY

Barth, R. (2001). *Learning By Heart* (p. 105). San Francisco, CA: Jossey-Bass.

Clark, R. (2011, June 17). Are You Using the Pinch Theory of Conflict Management? [Weblog]. Retrieved 13 August 2016, from http://tkographix.com/are-you-using-thepinch-theory-of-conflict-management/

DuFour, R., & Eaker, R. (1998). *Professional Learning Communities at Work: Best Practices for Enhancing Student Achievement.* Bloomington, IN: Solution Tree Press.

Edmondson, A. C. (2012). *Teaming: How Organizations Learn, Innovate, and Compete in the Knowledge Economy.* San Francisco, CA: Jossey-Bass.

Garmston, R., & B. Wellman (2013). *The Adaptive School: A Sourcebook for Collaborative Groups.* (2nd ed.). Plymouth: Rowan and Littlefield Publishers.

Lencioni, P. (2002). *The Five Dysfunctions of Teams: A Leadership Fable.* San Francisco, CA: Jossey-Bass.

Little, J. W. (1982). Norms of collegiality and experimentation: Workplace conditions of school success. *American Educational Research Journal*, 19(3), 325–340. http://doi.org/10.3102/00028312019003325

Klein, G. (2007). Performing a Project Premortem. *Harvard Business Review*, 85(9), 18-19.

Manktelow, J., & Brodbeck, F. (2009). *Team Tools: Build and Lead an Exceptional Team* [ebook]. London: Mind Tools Limited. Retrieved from https://www.mindtools.com/.

Nandagopal, A. (2013, 7 June 2013). 4 Reasons Why Teamwork Matters. [Weblog]. Retrieved 9 August 2016, from http://www.pickyourgoals.com/productivity/teamwork/

Pink, D. (2011). *Drive: The Surprising Truth About What Motivates Us.* New York, NY: Penguin Group.

Rath, T., & Conchie, B. (2009). *Strengths Based Leadership: Great Leaders, Teams, and Why People Follow.* New York, NY: Gallup Press.

Senge, P. M., Cambron-McCabe, N., Lucas, T., Smith, B., Dutton J., Kleiner, A. (2012). *Schools That Learn (Updated and Revised): A Fifth Discipline Fieldbook for Educators, Parents, and Everyone Who Cares About Education.* New York, NY: Crown Publishing Group.

Shmoker, M. (2006a). *Focus: Elevating the Essentials to Radically Improve Student Learning.* Alexandria, VA: Association for Supervision and Curriculum Development.

Shmoker, M. (2006b). *Results Now: How We Can Achieve Unprecedented Improvements in Teaching and Learning.* Alexandria, VA: Association for Supervision and Curriculum Development.

Towery, T. L. (1995). *The Wisdom of Wolves : Nature's Way to Organizational Success* (p. 18). Franklin, TN: Wessex House Publishing.

Tuckman, B. W. (1965). Developmental sequence in small groups. *Psychological Bulletin*, 63(6): 384-399.

SECTION 2

EXPLORING THE NUTS & BOLTS OF INSTRUCTIONAL LEADERSHIP

Learning Targets

WHY LEARNING TARGETS ARE SO IMPORTANT

THE CHARACTERISTICS OF LEARNING TARGETS

CREATING A "NO SECRETS" CLASSROOM THROUGH THE USE OF LEARNING TARGETS

THE FOUNDATION FOR STUDENT-ENGAGED ASSESSMENT

WRITING LEARNING TARGETS

> "*The most effective teaching and the most meaningful student learning happen when teachers design the right learning target for today's lesson and use it along with their students to aim for and assess understanding.*"
>
> Connie Moss & Susan Brookhart (2012)

WHY LEARNING TARGETS ARE SO IMPORTANT

For instructional leaders the learning target is the alpha and omega of every conversation. When observing a lesson, the first thing instructional leaders should ask the teacher in a pre- and post-observation conference is "What is the learning target of this lesson?" During the observation, they should ask themselves "Is it clear or am I sitting here wondering what this lesson is about?" If you are wondering, chances are that the children are wondering as well. No one can meet a target they are unsure of. Instructional leaders are observing how students know what the target is and how well they understand what is expected of them. Every assessment that takes place throughout the lesson is in response to the learning target. Without a clear learning target, assessments become meaningless. All instructional experiences should directly correlate with student mastery of the learning target. In a post-observation conference, skilled instructional leaders ask teachers to bring evidence of student work created during the lesson, so that the teacher and observer can discuss where the students are in their level of mastery compared to the learning target. The learning target of any lesson is the foundation for everything else that follows. It is the first principle for meaningful learning and effective teaching (Moss & Brookhart, 2012).

Without a clearly written, defined, and discussed learning target there is no clarity or form to a lesson. There is nothing to assess student mastery against, because the target has never been defined. Activities become time fillers, because there is no evident reason why students are doing what they are doing. Learning targets are the first step in providing effective instruction, which in turn supports student achievement. This leads to meaningful learning for every student. Learning targets provide the necessary meaning, focus, and roadmap for assessment, reflection, and modification of teaching and learning on a daily basis.

In addition, learning targets empower students to reflect upon their current level of mastery and compare it to the target. They can design their own ways to reach the target and the steps that will enable them to do so. For students the learning targets become the driving force that helps them build their own voice, reflect on their accomplishments, and set their own path to learning. Thanks to the continued use of learning targets student engagement and ownership of their learning has a secondary effect of raising their motivation for the mastery of knowledge, which, in turn, leads them gradually toward success. Confidence, joy, achievement, and investment all grow because of the use of learning targets (Berger, Rugen & Woodfin, 2014).

Learning targets help to distinguish one lesson from another, gauge student progress and success, give planning lessons a focus, and align instructional delivery (*Figure 1*).

Chapter 5 / Learning Targets

Figure 1. The role of learning targets in effective teaching (adapted from Moss & Brookhart, 2012)

THE CHARACTERISTICS OF LEARNING TARGETS

For learning targets to be useful for students, they must be written in a studentfriendly language. More specifically, they need to be clear and concise, and not intimidating. They need to be written in the form of "I can..." statements, so that students can feel they own the target. The targets are written for one single lesson but are linked to past and future lessons as well. They are designed to support the standards (such as the Common Core) and the students. An effective teacher makes time to discuss the learning targets with their students before the lesson begins and makes sure that every single student understands what they are to learn.

Defining a learning target is not an act of compliance to get the principal off one's back, but rather an important "I can" statement of empowerment which is referred to throughout the lesson and the closure of the lesson to see if students can indeed do what is being asked of them. The learning target is measurable. As a result, students can assess whether they have mastered it or not. The learning target becomes the compass which guides student self-assessment and reflection. Ideally, every teacher in every classroom should be able to say: "I can write learning targets and criteria for assessing if they have been achieved".

In Table 1 below notice the wording of learning targets as found in Berger's, Rugen's and Woodfin's book *Leaders of Their Own Learning* (2014). They all begin with "I can...". The idea is for the students to own their success as they master each learning target. They name the specific skill they are to acquire, which gives the purpose and focus to every lesson and activity.

Learning targets for younger students	Learning targets for older students
• I can describe the differences between living and non-living things.	• I can show two variable data on a scatter plot.
• I can explain my reasons for sorting and classifying insects	• I can describe how photosynthesis and cellular respiration help an ecosystem maintain homeostasis.
• I can find words I want to use in books, word walls, and word cards.	• I can describe historical events that affected the Sacco and Vanzetti case using a primary source text.
• I can write words that send a message.	

Table 1. Examples of daily learning targets (from Berger, Rugen & Woodfin, 2014)

CREATING A "NO SECRETS" CLASSROOM THROUGH THE USE OF LEARNING TARGETS

Students often don't know the purpose of the lesson or why they are asked to learn "it", whatever this "it" may be. They don't know what is expected of them. They don't know the reasons for the activities they are engaged in, except that the teacher has asked them to do it, and they don't know how they will be assessed or graded. They don't know what the finished product is supposed to look like or what the criteria for success are. It is all one big secret. As a result, students don't know what to focus on, reflect upon, or what to study to move on to the next step. The teacher has all the power, and the students are in the dark.

In a "no secrets" classroom — which is what every classroom should be — students know what they should learn or be able to do at the end of the lesson. It is written in the form of a learning target and referred to throughout the lesson. The learning target is discussed with the students, and they are asked to explain it back to see whether they understand what is being asked of them. Teachers know that just because they've explained the learning target, it doesn't necessarily mean that the students understand what they need to do. Formatively assessing their understanding of the learning target is a critical step. If students don't understand the target, it is impossible to reach it.

In a "no secrets" classroom students get to know the criteria against which they measure their success in achieving the learning target. They are also given specific examples of successful performance, so they don't have to guess what is on the teacher's mind. This guessing game is unfair and diminishes psychological safety and trust in the teacher.

THE FOUNDATION FOR STUDENT-ENGAGED ASSESSMENT

Learning targets help students to embrace assessment as something they can do on their own as opposed to something that is being done to them. Because students understand what the learning target is, they know how to prepare and study for an assessment of their mastery. Students can compare their work with exemplars, reflect on any gaps in their learning, design goals, create action steps, reflect again, and continue learning. This process, which begins with clear learning targets, fosters a culture of student efficacy. Learning targets and criteria for success enable students to deepen their engagement with content, to reflect and revise, and to help their classmates achieve mastery as well.

Figure 2 illustrates the process of planning, reflection, and adjustment when gaps in learning are assessed against the learning target.

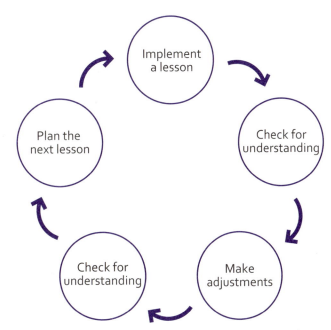

Figure 2. Adjusting instruction based on gaps in understanding (Berger, Rugen & Woodfin 2014).

WRITING LEARNING TARGETS

Driven by the standards such as Common Core, learning targets are specific to each lesson. Connie Moss and Susan Brookhart (2012) remind us that no matter how beautifully a learning target is written, if it is asking students to learn something that is unimportant, not aligned with a standard, or not involving a level of academic rigor, it is an ineffective learning target. We want to support teachers who plan for and teach a rigorous lesson that is a stretch but an attainable one, as described with Vygotsky's zone of proximal development (1978). A good question to ask ourselves is "Is this an effective learning target?"

In pursuit of academic rigor, familiarizing yourself with Norman Webb's depth of knowledge levels (2002) can help a lot in defining learning targets. For example, level one means the student can recall information; level two means skills and/or concepts have been acquired; level three involves strategic thinking such as reasoning, planning, using evidence, and explaining oneself; and level four involves extended thinking, that is, complex reasoning, planning, and developing over an extended period of time. Most learning targets focus on levels one through three.

Learning targets can also overlap over a school year if they are after building the character of students (responsibility, revision, inquiry, perspective taking, collaboration, leadership, service, and stewardship) (Berger, Rugen & Woodfin, 2014). Some learning targets might address the sixteen habits of mind defined by Arthur Costa and Bena Kallick (2009), such as questioning and problem posing or managing impulsivity. The reality is that whenever the learning target is known, the students are much more apt to reach it. Even more so if the target is attainable, understandable, and written in the "I can…" form. After all, isn't this our goal?

WHAT THIS LOOKS LIKE IN YOUR SCHOOL

1. Teachers write down learning targets for daily lessons on white and blackboards and are referred to throughout the lesson.

2. Teachers conduct activities that are specifically devised to achieve the learning targets.

3. Teachers check with students if they understand what the learning targets are.

4. Students and teachers reflect on the evidence of student performance in view of the learning targets.

5. Teachers modify and personalize lessons based on the evidence of student performance in view of the learning targets.

6. Students are asked to articulate what they're learning based on their understanding of the learning targets.

7. Students can support each other in meeting the learning targets.

8. Students track their learning progress and design goals and action plans based on the learning targets.

9. Learning targets and assessments are aligned with the standards to create a coherent lesson and unit.

10. Teachers plan together and discuss the consistency and coherence of their learning targets with each other.

Building Your Instructional Leadership

STRATEGIES TO TRY
USING LEARNING TARGETS AS A FOUNDATION FOR EFFECTIVE INSTRUCTION

1. Practice not just reading but also discussing the learning targets with students, so that they understand them, are motivated to pursue them, and are more apt to achieve them.

2. Write down learning targets that focus on a skill or concept instead of simply describing an activity (i.e., complete the worksheet).

3. Write down longer-term learning targets that are tied to curriculum standards and take two weeks to complete and the short-term learning targets that strategically lead you to achieve the longer-term targets.

4. Post, discuss, and use learning targets on a daily basis. Teachers and the administrators can reflect on the use of learning targets by using the rubric below (*Table 2*).

5. Set the criteria against which you can assess whether the learning targets have been achieved.

6. Correlate the essence of each standard with "I can…" learning target statements to see whether they support the standard.

7. Watch the video "Students discuss the power of learning targets"[1] with your teacher colleagues and discuss the implications for your planning and interactions.

8. Watch the video "Using a learning target throughout the lesson"[2] with your teacher colleagues and discuss the implications for your planning and interactions.

9. Watch the video "Students unpack a learning target"[3] with your teacher colleagues and discuss the implications for your planning and interactions.

---

1 available at: https://vimeo.com/44052220
2 available at: https://vimeo.com/44052221
3 available at: https://vimeo.com/44052219

Chapter 5 / Learning Targets

	Accomplished	Developing	Beginning
Standards-based and rigorous	They are derived from national or state standards and school or district documents such as curriculum maps and adopted program materials. Targets fall across multiple categories in a cognitive rigor matrix.	They are derived from general academic tasks but not grade-specific standards, or they describe learning or tasks that do not meet proficiency standards. Targets fall across limited categories in a cognitive rigor matrix.	They are not derived from standards and do not clearly reference academic tasks. Targets fall primarily in one or two columns/rows of a cognitive rigor matrix, or learning targets are not rigorous enough.
Student-friendly	They are written in studentfriendly language (accessible vocabulary and from a student perspective) and begin with the stem "I can".	They begin with the stem "I can" but may not use student-friendly language; i.e., they sound like "objectives."	They do not begin with "I can" and/or are simply reiterations of state objectives.
Measurable	They are measurable and use concrete, assessable verbs (e.g., identify, compare, analyze). The verb suggests the way in which the target will be assessed (e.g., "analyze" suggests a writing or problem-solving assessment, not a multiple choice quiz).	They are measurable but may contain two verbs or have too broad a scope in content (e.g., I can draw a raccoon and describe its habitat).	They are not measurable (e.g., I can understand, or I can commit).
Specific and contextualized	They are specific, often referring to the particular context of a lesson, project, or case study.	They articulate only longterm targets that can be generalized for any similar academic task (e.g., I can write a persuasive essay).	They are too broad for students to see progress (e.g., I can read) or too narrow for students to own their learning (e.g. I can put my name on my paper).
Learning-centered	The verb following the "I can" stem clearly identifies the intended learning, articulating what the students will learn rather than how they will demonstrate their learning.	They verb following the "I can" stem focuses on the academic tasks students will do rather than what students will learn (e.g., I can complete a graphic organizer).	The targets are focused only on compliance and completion (e.g., I can retake my test).

Table 2. Learning targets rubric
Adopted from Expeditionary Learning[4]

---

[4] available at: http://commons.eleducation.org/sites/default/files/Learning%20target%20rubric_EL_110812_1.pdf

BIBLIOGRAPHY

Berger, R., Rugen, L., & Woodfin, L. (2014). *Leaders of Their Own Learning*. San Francisco, CA: Wiley and Sons.

Costa, A., & Kallick, B. (Eds.) (2009). *Learning and Leading with Habits of Mind: 16 Essential Characteristics for Success*. Alexandria, VA: Association for Supervision and Curriculum Development.

Davies, A. (2011). *Making Classroom Assessment Work* (3rd ed.). Courtenay, BC: Connections Publishing and Bloomington, IN: Solution Tree Press.

Moss, C., & Brookhart, S. (2012). *Learning Targets: Helping Students Aim for Understanding in Today's Lesson*. Alexandria, VA: Association for Supervision and Curriculum Development.

Vygotsky, L. S. (1978). *Mind in Society: The Development of Higher Psychological Processes*. Cambridge, MA: Harvard University Press.

Webb, N. (2002). *Combined Webb Depth of Knowledge Levels for Mathematics*. Alexandria, VA: National Assessment of Educational Progress.

Wiggins, G., & McTighe J. (2005). *Understanding by Design* (2nd ed.). Alexandria, VA: Association for Supervision and Curriculum Development.

Looking for Proof: Evidence of Student Learning

ALL ROADS LEAD TO STUDENT ACHIEVEMENT

A SHIFT FROM WHAT IS TAUGHT TO WHAT IS LEARNED

THE TRIPLE A THEORY

COGNITIVE EMPATHY

THE DIFFERENCE BETWEEN FORMATIVE AND SUMMATIVE ASSESSMENT

LOOKING FOR PROOF THROUGH FORMATIVE ASSESSMENT

MAKING THINKING VISIBLE AS A MEANS OF FORMATIVE ASSESSMENT

WHAT TO DO WITH THE EVIDENCE ONCE YOU HAVE COLLECTED IT

HOW FORMATIVE ASSESSMENT INFORMS PLANNING AND INSTRUCTIONS

> "*The key features of effective learning environments are that they create student engagement and allow teachers, learners, and their peers to ensure that the learning is proceeding in the intended direction. The only way we can do this is through assessment. That is why assessment is, indeed, the bridge between teaching and learning.*"
>
> Dylan Wiliam, *Embedded Formative Assessment* (2011)

ALL ROADS LEAD TO STUDENT ACHIEVEMENT

As instructional leaders, our ultimate focus is on student learning and student achievement. We care deeply about creating an environment of empathy, psychological safety, and trust, so that students can feel supported, appreciated, and in a cognitively safe place to do their best learning. For instructional leaders learning targets are critical as the baseline for the ongoing measurement of student learning and achievement. Learning targets are only one bookend of the pair. They create focus and clearly identify the goal of what students need to know or be able to do. The other bookend is to find out where the students currently stand in respect to that learning goal, so that instruction can be modified accordingly. Tangible evidence of student learning (student work, conversations, and alternative forms of data) creates the opportunity for assessment for both teacher and student. It encourages reflection, revision of goals, and next steps to support students in increasing their learning and achievement.

A SHIFT FROM WHAT IS TAUGHT TO WHAT IS LEARNED

Consistent checking for students' current level of understanding is a shift in paradigm from an emphasis on teaching to an emphasis on learning. Historically, instructional leaders observed teachers to assess teaching methodology, the content that was taught, and whether the students were engaged and on task. A skilled instructional leader today looks for evidence of students learning and of teachers focusing on understanding and formative assessment embedded in a lesson (Wiliam, 2011). Every lesson should have some kind of demonstration of proficiency in response to the stated learning target (Davies, 2011).

This paradigm shift also addresses how teachers interact with each other as they support student learning and student achievement. Historically, teachers had been isolated, individually studying standards and trying to figure out how to unpack and transfer them into specific daily lesson plans. In the name of student learning, teachers now work in teams, creating a common language and understanding of learning targets and standards. Teachers now form teams to study student work. Instructional leaders ask teachers to study demonstrations of proficiency to see how they affect lesson planning, reflection, and skill-based regrouping and re-teaching.

Instructional leaders now know that the shift is clearly student-centered, with students doing most of the talking and most of the work. The days of a teachercentered, lecture-based classroom are over. The more a teacher talks, the more they rob each student of an opportunity to transform learning into a personal experience. It is the act of transformation which makes learning personal, which in turn transfers learning into long-term memory. Teacher-centered classrooms violate brain research findings about how students transform information to move learning into long-term memory. I love the title of Robyn Jackson's book *Never Work Harder Than Your Students* (2009) for exactly this reason. If teachers are doing all the talking, students do not get the chance to show their current understanding. The ultimate goal of the paradigm shift is to get evidence of student learning, so that students can build their own sense of self-direction and cultivate themselves as leaders of their own learning (Berger, Rugen & Woodfin, 2014).

THE TRIPLE A THEORY

The current view of formative assessment is in support of what I call the "triple A theory". The first "A" is *assessment*. To truly understand the student's current level of understanding, we need to assess it in a multitude of ways. Embedded formative assessment strategies, activator and summarizer strategies, student conferences, informal conversations, and written responses to a number of different prompts all provide a number of data points for teachers to contemplate.

However, just having a lot of data points is meaningless unless teachers act on the second "A" in this theory, which is *analysis*. It's the reflection on these data points that is critical. Teachers should ask themselves: "What are the patterns and trends that are emerging from the data I just collected from my class?".

Once they have truly dug into and identified the skills and learning targets with which the students are struggling, teachers can move to the third "A", which is *adaptation*. It is the analysis which leads to the adaptation of the plans that teachers may have considered foolproof. The passage from analysis to adaptation keeps educators intellectually humble. It is not enough to assess and it is not enough to think about it. Ultimately, skilled teachers adapt their lesson plans, their methodologies, and what they had thought was working based on the data that tell them their students have trouble acquiring knowledge.

Skilled instructional leaders, for their part, encourage this kind of reflective, datadriven approach in their teachers. They ask every teacher to bring the collected student work and other data from the lesson which was just observed. They assist each teacher in the analysis and adaptation as they look at the data together. Together they analyze which students have met the target, which students exceeded the target, and which students are in a "not yet" position in terms of their mastery. They discuss which instructional strategies are necessary to remove the obstacles to student learning. Instructional leaders expect teachers to modify their instruction in the name of student learning and student achievement. Just because the teacher covered content, this does not mean a student has mastered it. We are consistently looking for proof.

COGNITIVE EMPATHY

An astute instructional leader knows that embedded formative assessment, the hunger for data showing the students' current mastery of knowledge, and a predisposition for looking for proof are based on a very big assumption. Many assume that all teachers embrace the concept of "cognitive empathy". Cognitive empathy means that as a teacher I want to make a specific effort to get into your head to understand your ways of acquiring knowledge (Goleman, 2002; Stueber, 2014). Cognitively empathic teachers seek to understand how each student learns best.

They want to figure out the learning styles and which auditory, visual, kinesthetic, and multiple intelligences approaches best reach their students. Cognitively empathic teachers see themselves and their role in support of students and their learning, not the other way around. The student is the client. In a cognitively empathic classroom the teacher seeks to meet the clients' needs.

Through hundreds of teacher observations I have learned that it is indeed an assumption to believe that every educator in every classroom embraces this concept. And yet, unless we embrace cognitive empathy, there is no need to collect evidence of student learning. The impetus to analyze student data to adapt instruction and the need to differentiate and personalize learning to support student mastery is tossed by the wayside. An instructional leader models cognitive empathy and expects teachers to do the same in every classroom.

THE DIFFERENCE BETWEEN FORMATIVE AND SUMMATIVE ASSESSMENT

Many people ask what is the difference between formative and summative assessment. There are two analogies that best provide an answer to that question. The gentler analogy talks about making a big pot of soup for the impending guests. As the chef is adding and stirring the ingredients, he or she is tasting along the way. The chef might decide that the soup needs a little more salt, a little more stock or that it's a bit too thin and will add more vegetables. Always checking and tasting, the chef will ultimately decide the soup is ready to be served. This process is formative assessment. Summative assessment starts with the guests. After they taste the soup, you can tell whether they like it or not from the looks on their faces and from whether they ask for seconds or not all. This is summative assessment. Formative assessment is ongoing, embedded in the process, and it gives the chef the opportunity to fix the soup if it's not quite right. Summative assessment means it's over. If the guests are gagging you know the soup did not go well. Because it is summative, it is too late to change it.

The more graphic analogy is a medical one: formative assessment is like taking the patient's temperature or blood pressure. They are still alive. If there is a dilemma, the doctor can still do something about it. Summative assessment is a post-mortem. The patient has passed away, and the doctors are trying to figure out what happened. Regardless, it is too late. The patient is gone and there is nothing else to do. Some teachers say that this analogy sounds like the "end-of-unit test". Half of the students flunked it, but the unit is over, and the teacher needs to move on in the curriculum.

Instructional leaders know that summative assessments are anti-climactic and after the fact. Skillful teachers spend most of their instructional efforts collecting formative assessments when the patient is still alive and they can still do something about it.

LOOKING FOR PROOF THROUGH FORMATIVE ASSESSMENT

David Sousa has identified two criteria for information to pass into long-term memory and thus be learned (2011). It must make sense to the learner and it must have meaning or be relevant. Formative assessment strategies such as phrases and prompts provide a way to help students begin to make both sense and meaning of new information. The first step of metacognition (raising students' awareness of what's going on in their heads) lays the foundation for students to be self-monitoring about their learning when compared to the identified learning targets. This real-time, informal data (as opposed to standardized tests which arrive at the end of the year, which is a year too late) provide valuable information to the teacher, who can more precisely target teaching interventions.

Anne Davies and her groundbreaking formative assessment work (Davies, 2011; Gregory, Cameron & Davies, 2011) support the brain research of David Sousa and the tenets of valuable formative assessment data for both teachers and students. Some of the formative assessment strategies are listed here.

Interacting-with-content strategies

Phrases and prompts

The teacher provides sentence stems such as those below to prompt students to think about their new information:

- The part I like best…
- What was confusing…
- Two things I learned…
- One question I have…
- I already knew about…
- One thing I know that wasn't mentioned is…
- I'd like to know more about…

Margin symbols

Students mark their notes or an assignment with symbols on the margins to comment on their level of understanding and mastery. Here are some examples:

! – this is too hard
✓ – this is easy for me
+ – I know this so well I can teach someone else
☺ – I need to do this with a partner
T – I need more time

Reflection cards

Another self-monitoring strategy, reflection cards structure ways for students to reflect on what they have learned as well as difficulties they have encountered. Here are some examples:

- *Muddiest point card*: "The muddiest point in _____ is _____."

- *Recall card*: List three points you remember from the last class.
- *Exit pass/slip*: "Two things I learned... One question I have..."
- *One-word web card* (a wheel-like graphic organizer in which the main word or concept is in the center and is connected with its descriptors or comments with spoke-like lines, see *Figure 1* for illustration)

Looking-for-proof strategies

These strategies give students an opportunity to assess their own products and performances with cards that have a word or a phrase that reflect their thoughts about a piece of work. Students then give reasons for their selection.

Proof cards

Using cards, students explain how the phrase applies to their product or performance. Here are some examples:

- *Favorite*: "This is my favorite part because..."
- *Trash it!*: "Two reasons this [part] should be trashed are..."
- *Perseverance*: "I really tried hard to..."
- *Potential*: "I plan to keep working on this because..."

Before-and-after proof

Students look at their learning over time by selecting specific examples that show evidence of their growth.

- "I used to _____ and now I _____"

Students make webs at the beginning of a unit to show what they know. At the end of the unit, students complete their web using a different color to show learning growth (*Figure 1*).

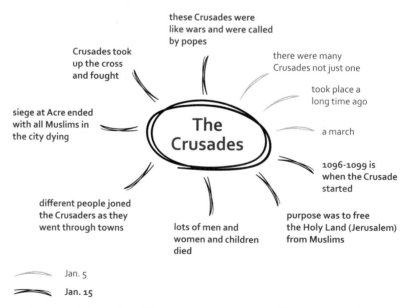

Figure 1. The role of learning targets in effective teaching
(adapted from Moss & Brookhart, 2012)

Personal records

Students keep personal records of what they are doing and learning as a way of showing evidence of their improvement and personal growth over time. Periodically, they can write summary comments about their learning. Here are some examples:

- Data notebooks
- Bookmarks
- Graphs
- Calendar records
- Quiz records

Connect-to-criteria strategies

Connect-to-criteria strategies give students the opportunity to compare their product or performance to criteria for success in order to improve their work.

Met/Not yet

Students assess their work against set criteria (specified in rubrics, exemplars, or checklists) and students and/or their peers determine whether they have met these criteria or not. They show or talk about the evidence that supports their verdict. They can also identify what in particular they would like their teacher to notice. Here's an example:

- *Highlighters*: students use color-coded highlighters (such as green for "met" and red for "not yet") to note where they have met criteria and areas for improvement.

Sample match

Teachers post samples of student work that meet criteria at different levels. Students then match their own work to the most similar sample. Students record specific reasons for the match they made.

Acronyms

After setting criteria with or for students, teacher and students decide on an acronym where each letter relates to a criterion statement. Here's an example:

- **WALL** criteria for posters: **W**ords are spelled correctly; **A**ccurate and key information is shown; **L**anguage is clear with no extra words; **L**ooks neat and eye-catching

MAKING THINKING VISIBLE AS A MEANS OF FORMATIVE ASSESSMENT

Project Zero of the Harvard Graduate School of Education has been providing very important foundations for teaching and building a culture of higher-level thinking for the last thirty years[1]. Over the last five years, Ron Ritchhart and colleagues have

---

[1] for more information visit http://www.pz.harvard.edu/

added to Project Zero a new body of research and practices they call Visible Thinking (2011). Visible Thinking brings a series of thinking routines that can be embedded in teacher's practice[2]. In addition to scaffolding higher-level thinking, every one of the strategies is a means of formative assessment that evidences student's understanding. Thinking is integral to understanding, which is being assessed, and the thinking routines include (Ritchhart, Church & Morrison, 2011, p. 11):

- Observing closely and describing what is there;
- Building explanations and interpretations;
- Reasoning with evidence;
- Making connections;
- Considering different viewpoints and perspectives; and
- Capturing the heart and forming conclusions.

Their strategies make the invisible (what is in the heads of the students) visible, so that teachers can reflect on and analyze their teaching and help students to understand the skills and concepts that are being learned. Specific routines ask students to dig deeper, make connections, and organize ideas. Instructional leader support teachers to incorporate these routines into their weekly instructional plans.

WHAT TO DO WITH THE EVIDENCE ONCE YOU HAVE COLLECTED IT

The point of collecting data in real time is to quickly review for trends and patterns of conceptual understanding. Some of the questions that a teacher or a team of teachers might pose are:

- What do these data suggest about what students know or have learned?
- What do these data reveal about students' abilities to apply the knowledge they have learned?
- What do these data show about what students value?
- Which students do you still not know much about?

The answers to these questions will guide conversations about instruction. The collected data suggest which instructional strategies have brought learning results and which have not. The data will surface which skills and concepts need more attention and which students need more help with the identified skill sets. The conversation leads teachers to discuss the effective teaching methods for the identified concepts. These methods then appear in revised lesson plans for the next day and week.

HOW FORMATIVE ASSESSMENT INFORMS PLANNING AND INSTRUCTION

As teachers plan differently and teach in different ways based on what the collected data suggest, Black & Wiliam (1998) have proposed five key premises on which

---

[2] available at: http://www.visiblethinkingpz.org/

formative assessment is based:

- Students are actively involved in their own learning processes;
- Effective feedback is provided to students;
- Students are able to perform self-assessments; and
- The influence of assessment on students motivation is recognized.

Starting from these premises, Black & William (2009) have also proposed strategies to be consistently included in both planning and instruction:

- clarifying and sharing learning intentions and criteria for success;
- engineering effective classroom discussions and other learning tasks that elicit evidence of student understanding; providing feedback that moves learners forward;
- activating students as instructional resources for one another; and
- activating students as the owners of their own learning

To use their own words: "Practice in a classroom is formative to the extent that evidence about student achievement is elicited, interpreted, used by teachers, learners, or their peers, to make decisions about the next steps in instruction that are likely to be better, or better founded, than the decisions they would have taken in the absence of the evidence that was elicited." (Black & William, 2009)

WHAT THIS LOOKS LIKE IN YOUR SCHOOL

As an instructional leader you should:

1. intentionally model the belief that everyone can get smarter through hard work, studying evidence of learning, receiving effective feedback, and practicing effective learning strategies.

2. emphasize the importance of the students' role in their own learning through student-centered classrooms, student self-assessments, student goal setting and action steps, and student-led conferences.

3. regularly observe all classrooms to analyze for consistency in checking for understanding and in using evidence to modify instruction

4. ask teachers to reflect on the presence of higher-level thinking embedded within lesson content provided on a daily basis based on collected evidence.

5. coach teachers to uphold classroom culture that invites mistakes as research and reflection opportunities and seeks to provide evidence of student learning on a daily basis.

6. require teachers to bring evidence of student learning that correlates with the learning targets for each observed lesson. This evidence will guide the postobservation discussion.

7. seek to expand the repertoire of learning assessment strategies for every teacher in every classroom (see the Looking for proof practices above), so that every day is not another "exit slip".

8. make post-observation conferences happen and provide teachers with strategies to sort student work against the criteria and exemplar.

9. support teachers in planning, so that they know how to address and modify their plans when gaps in student learning present themselves.

10. plan a collaboration session for the faculty to discuss alternative instructional methods to address trends in learning gaps at the grade, team, or department level.

STRATEGIES TO TRY

BUILDING FACULTY SKILLS IN COLLECTING EVIDENCE OF STUDENT LEARNING

1. Practice writing pre-planning strategic questions; e. g., provide a clear vision of the learning target; scaffold questions from basic to complex, or clarify expectations.

2. Practice using student discussion protocols which engage all students and provide formative assessment data for teachers. Some student discussion protocols include (Berger, 2014):

   - *Back-to-back* and face-to-face protocol. Partners stand back to back and wait for the prompt from the teacher. The teacher signals that they should face each other and each student takes turns speaking and listening.

   - *Carousel brainstorming*. Students are divided into small groups. Different questions are posted on chart paper around the room. Each group brainstorms what they know and write down their reply to that question with their own color marker for a set amount of time. Then each group moves to the next station to repeat the process with the next question.

   - *Write-pair-switch*. Students begin by working alone on a prompt. Then they share what they have written with the student sitting next to them. In the final step, partners are changed and everyone shares with the person sitting in front or behind.

3. *No opt out*. This strategy which requires each student to give a correct answer to the question. Make use of the helpful ideas from Quality Questioning by Jackie Walsh and Beth Sattes (2005) such as cues to help students recall, clues, hints or overt reminders, probing for reasoning behind an incorrect answer, rephrasing the same question in different words. If the answer is still incorrect, the teacher turns to a next student until she or he gets the correct answer. Then the teacher returns to the first student or any subsequent student who did not know the answer, so they get an opportunity to restate or repeat the correct answer.

4. When checking for understanding during instructional time, guide students to analyze their learning patterns, the logic of their reasoning, and their ability to apply their learning in new situations by asking probing questions such as:

   - Why do you think of this?
   - How do you know?
   - What evidence supports your thinking?
   - activating students as instructional resources for one another; and
   - How has your thinking changed and what changed your ideas?

5. As a team or department, practice using the Tuning Protocol (*Table 1*) to identify the strengths and weaknesses of an anonymous model of student work.

> ### The Tuning Protocol
>
> **Purpose**: to identify the strengths and weaknesses of an anonymous work model
> **Time**: approximately 30 minutes
> **Grade level**: fifth and higher
> **Roles**: presenter or teacher, participants (ideally in small groups)
> **Steps**:
>
> 1. *Presentation by presenter or teacher; participants are silent (four minutes)*
>   - Provide context for the work being discussed.
>   - Present a question to the group that will help them focus their feedback on one aspect
>
> 2. *Reading and examination (three to eight minutes)*
>   Students examine the work, focusing on the question the presenter or teacher asked.
>
> 3. *Clarifying questions (three minutes)*
>   Clarifying questions are matter of fact; save substantive issues for later. Clarifying questions are answerable with "yes," "no," or a single brief sentence. The teacher or presenter is responsible for making sure that clarifying questions are truly clarifying in nature.
>
> 4. *Processing by participants (ten to fifteen minutes)*
>   Participants talk to each other about the teacher's or presenter's work, with particular attention to the focusing question, whereas the teacher or presenter remains quiet, taking notes as appropriate. The group begins dialogue by concentrating on the following:
>   - Strengths
>   - Disconnects and problems
>   - Questions for probing or further reflection on the part of the presenter
>
> 5. *Teacher's or presenter's response (five minutes)*
>   Presenter shares significant points, recognizes powerful feedback, and identifies next steps.

Table 1. The Tuning Protocol
(from Berger, Ruger & Woodfin, 2014, p. 146)

6. Support students in setting their own goals using the sample goal-setting worksheet (*Table 2*). Ask them to discuss their goals and action steps to meet their goals with each other.

Goal-Setting Worksheet

Name: _____   Week Ending: _____

Weekly Reflection

A target I am working on this week is:

[🎯]   [_____]

A goal I have around the target is:
_____
_____
_____

I think I have made little/some/great progress towards my goal and the learning target because:
_____
_____
_____

ON TIME
Home Learning
Return Rate: [____] %

I am/am not missing any work.
(Missing assignments are listed below.)
_____
_____

Teacher initials: _____   Parent signature: _____

Comments?
_____
_____

Table 2. An example of a goal-setting worksheet
(from Berger, Rugen & Woodfin, 2014, p. 117)

7. As a team or department, practice using the LAST Protocol (Looking at Student Thinking)[3] against a set of student work to discuss next steps for your instruction.

8. Practice strategic observation and listening to determine the needs for small and whole-group instruction.

9. Watch the video "Best Practices: Checking for Understanding"[4] and reflect on how these strategies correlate with your current practice (4 minutes, 40 seconds).

---

3   available at: http://www.ronritchhart.com/COT_Resources.html
4   available at: https://www.youtube.com/watch?v=atTFFzcvqfE

10. Watch the video "Instructional Strategies that Support Learning – Checking for Understanding"[5] and reflect on how these strategies correlate with your current practice (5 minutes, 33 seconds).

---

[5] available at: https://www.youtube.com/watch?v=bMlbNk4gZ5U

BIBLIOGRAPHY

Berger, R., Rugen, L., & Woodfin, L. (2014). *Leaders of Their Own Learning*. San Francisco, CA: Wiley and Sons.

Black, P., & Wiliam, D. (1998). Assessment and Classroom Learning. *Assessment in Education: Principles, Policy & Practice*, 5(1), 7-74. doi: 10.1080/0969595980050102

Black, P., & Wiliam, D. (2009). Developing the Theory of Formative Assessment. *Educational Assessment, Evaluation and Accountability* 21(1), 5–31. doi:10.1007/s11092-008-9068-5

Davies, A. (2011). *Making Classroom Assessment Work* (3rd ed.). Courtenay, BC: Connections Publishing and Bloomington, IN: Solution Tree Press.

DuFour, Richard, DuFour, Rebecca, Eaker, R., & Many, T. (2006). *Learning by Doing: A Handbook for Professional Learning Communities at Work*. Bloomington, IN: Solution Tree Press.

Goleman, D., Boyatzis, R. E., & McKee, A. (2002). *Primal Leadership: Realizing the Power of Emotional Intelligence*. Boston, MA.: Harvard Business School Press.

Gregory, K., Cameron, C., & Davies, A. (2011). *Knowing what counts: Self-assessment and goal setting* (2nd ed.). Bloomington, IN: Solution Tree Press.

Gregory, K., Cameron, C., & Davies, A. (1997). *Setting and Using Criteria*. Courtenay, BC: Building Connections Publishing.

Hattie, J. (2012). *Visible Learning for Teachers: Maximizing Impact on Learning*. New York, NY: Routledge.

Jackson, R. (2009). *Never Work Harder Than Your Students & Other Principles of Great Teaching*. Alexandria, VA: Association for Supervision and Curriculum Development.

Ritchhart, R., Church, M., & Morrison, K. (2011). *Making Thinking Visible: How to Promote Engagement, Understanding, and Independence for All Learners*. San Francisco, CA: Jossey-Bass.

Sousa, A. D. (2011). *How the Brain Learns* (4th ed.). Thousand Oaks, CA: Corwin.

Stueber, K. (2014). The Study of Cognitive Empathy and Empathic Accuracy. In Zalta E. N. (Ed.), *The Stanford Encyclopedia of Philosophy* (Winter 2014 ed.). Retrieved from: http://plato.stanford.edu/entries/empathy/cognitive.html

Walsh, J. A., & Sattes, B. D. (2005). *Quality Questioning: Research-Based Practice to Engage Every Learner*. Thousand Oaks, CA: Corwin.

Wiliam, D., & Thompson, M. (2007). Integrating assessment with instruction: What will it take to make it work? In Dwyer, C. A. (Ed.). *The Future of Assessment: Shaping Teaching and Learning* (pp. 53–82). Mahwah, NJ: Erlbaum.

Wiliam, D. (2011). *Embedded Formative Assessment*. Bloomington, IN: Solution Tree Press.

Giving Descriptive Feedback

CATEGORIES OF RESPONSES
WHY DESCRIPTIVE FEEDBACK IS SO IMPORTANT
CRITICAL ASPECTS OF DESCRIPTIVE FEEDBACK
CREATING A CULTURE OF DESCRIPTIVE FEEDBACK
WAYS TO PROVIDE DESCRIPTIVE FEEDBACK

> *I think it's very important to have a feedback loop, where you're constantly thinking about what you've done and how you could be doing it better. I think that's the single best piece of advice: constantly think about how you could be doing things better and questioning yourself.*
>
> Elon Musk (founder, CEO, and product architect of Tesla Motors)

CATEGORIES OF RESPONSES

Put yourself back in time to when you were a student yourself in elementary, middle, and high school. If you have children of your own, you may also think about them as you replay this movie in your mind. Envision all of the worksheets, quizzes, tests, book reports, and research papers that were handed back to you by your teachers or that your children brought home for your review. Remember the kinds of comments that were written on these papers. They usually fell into one of five categories. The first category usually came in the form of symbols and pictures such as smiley faces, checks or check plus or minus signs, question marks or stickers with images of superheroes with lightning bolts or cartoon bubbles with words like "Shazam!", "Wowza!", and "Awesome!". The second category of response came in the form of numbers, like fractions (48/100; 92/100; 4/5; 3/10), percentages (72%; 98%; 50%), or numbers of incorrect questions (-5; -24; -13). The third category came in the form of letters (A+; B-; F; D+), the fourth category in the form of teacher-centered, egocentric comments or questions, such as "This is the best lab report you ever did! Keep up the good work", "I loved how creative you were", "When will you finally use gender agreements with the nouns?", "See me", "Did you study?", or "Are you kidding?". The last category came in one-word format which suggested the papers were reviewed in some way: "Clear", "Thorough", "Incomplete", "Elaborate", "Name?".

The reality is that none of these categories of responses count as feedback. They are some kind of response. They suggest that teachers have looked at the paper and interacted with the student's work in some way, but none of these categories and none of these comments are descriptive feedback. Teacher-centered responses such as the ones listed above simply tell you if you are in the doghouse or not, if your teacher is pleased or not, or if you handed in your work or not. Descriptive feedback is such a powerful tool for student learning and student achievement that every instructional leader must be able to analyze the characteristics of descriptive feedback and know the difference between descriptive feedback and teachercentered response, which does not provide any feedback at all.

WHY DESCRIPTIVE FEEDBACK IS SO IMPORTANT

The world's leading researchers in the area of descriptive feedback such as Wiggins, Black, Wiliam, Brookhart, Hattie, the Bellons, Blank, and Berger have all concluded that effective feedback makes a tremendous difference for student achievement between the classes where it is practiced and those where it isn't. Descriptive feedback provided to students in a consistent way has the power of raising levels of learning by 21-41 achievement points. Moreover, descriptive feedback is more strongly and consistently related to achievement than any other teaching behavior. According to Bellon, Bellon & Blank (1992, pp. 277–278), "...this relationship is consistent regardless of grade, socioeconomic status, race, or school setting. When feedback and corrective procedures are used, most students can attain the same level of achievement as the top 20% of students." Imagine a student entering the classroom with a mediocre level of understanding and concluding the course with total mastery simply by being the recipient of consistent descriptive feedback. The implications are profound for learners as well as for the teaching methods and teacher coaching by instructional leaders.

CRITICAL ASPECTS OF DESCRIPTIVE FEEDBACK

Instructional leaders need to be explicit as they explain to their faculty the elements of descriptive feedback, so that they can look for these elements in what teachers communicate to students and their parents as they return student's work. Instructional leaders should coach their faculty to provide constant and consistent descriptive feedback to students and should provide professional learning opportunities to clarify and support it.

Descriptive — and thus effective — feedback has three elements:

1. Recognition of the desired goal/standard of performance
2. Evidence of the current position in relation to the goal/standard
3. Some understanding of the way to close the gap between the two — a system of corrective procedures (Black & Wiliam, 1998)

It starts with providing a clear vision of what is being expected and what we need to attain using tangible models, such as work samples, video clips, and examples of products. When instructional leaders and teachers follow this format, the feedback is about the work. It is not personal or affective to the person who created the work. It is objective about the product or performance. Descriptive feedback is specific to the pre-designed learning target and to the success criteria. It spells out every element which should be present in the work. Whether the reviewer personally loved it or not is irrelevant to the work. In other words, "...good feedback is descriptive of the work and the process used to do the work, not the learner" (Moss & Brookhart, 2012). Teachers and instructional leaders who are committed to providing descriptive feedback are equally committed to providing clarity of expectation through success criteria and exemplars, and the feedback is directly and consistently correlated with those preestablished standards.

CREATING A CULTURE OF DESCRIPTIVE FEEDBACK

Instructional leaders expect of teachers to provide consistent feedback. The essential starting point for every feedback is to stay focused on these dispositions:

- Be kind.
- Be specific.
- Be helpful.

As recipients of these dispositions, teachers are more apt to consciously embrace and support a shift in paradigm which focuses on student learning, student mastery, high expectations, and self-reflection. They have experienced how valuable this process can be. When teachers provide feedback to students, they are expected to consciously remove themselves (and in some cases issues of ego and control) from the feedback equation. Instead, meaningful feedback relies on the success criteria, models, and exemplars. All comments respond directly to this baseline, not to a teacher's opinion, personal reaction, or judgmental response.

In addition, this paradigm shift may take many different directions. Historically, it was the instructional leader who gave feedback to the teacher. It was the teacher who gave responses (rarely feedback) to the students. That was where the potential for conversation and reflection ended. Now, the power of descriptive feedback is such that it can spread in many different ways. They all can improve student learning and student achievement. For one, teachers continue to provide descriptive feedback to students. In a student-centered classroom where students are groomed to be leaders of their own learning, and teachers see themselves as facilitators of student learning, students are also invited to provide descriptive feedback to teachers about their craft. Teachers appreciate this dialogue, as they learn which methods their students find helpful and supportive and which not as much. This enables teachers to hone their planning and methodological choices with the best interest of their students in mind. Another feedback option includes students providing descriptive feedback to each other. As soon as they are taught the basic rules of descriptive feedback (the same rules and models the teachers have learned from their instructional leaders), they can form groups providing feedback about the work their fellow students have produced. They are trained to provide specific comments about the work, directly tied to the success criteria and exemplar and to suggest steps to move this work closer to the expected level of mastery.

This paradigm shift expands not only by supporting students to be leaders of their own learning, but also by supporting teachers to collaborate and learn from each other in professional learning communities and other peer structures of interaction. This includes teachers being trained in how to provide descriptive feedback to each other about their planning and teaching, about the work generated by their students, and about teaching modifications based on the analysis of student work. It is a kind of laser-focused upgrade to an old model of peer observation. Teachers only provide objective (as opposed to opinion- or judgment-driven) information about the work, process, or content that has jointly been discussed before an observation or interaction. The descriptive feedback correlates to the information about accepted teacher standards, professional growth systems, curriculum documents, or success criteria.

Perhaps the biggest paradigm shift of all is that now instructional leaders invite and appreciate descriptive feedback from their faculty based on pre-established criteria and leadership goals communicated to the faculty. It models important two-way communication, reflection, vulnerability, trust, and continuous learning. Isn't that what we always want to be modeling for our faculty? Inviting feedback consistently (e. g. quarterly) is a powerful way to open, honest, two-way dialogue and reflection.

Chapter 7 / Giving Descriptive Feedback

WAYS TO PROVIDE DESCRIPTIVE FEEDBACK

Feedback can be provided in three steps, starting with what students are doing well, followed by what needs improvement, and concluding with the specific steps to make that improvement a reality (Davies, 2007, p. 2).

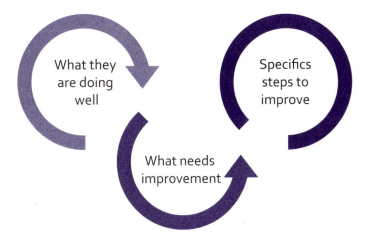

Figure 1. The three steps of descriptive feedback

Feedback can also be provided by using a criteria-for-success form such as the one presented in Figure 2. Students can share their perceptions with teachers. They can discuss where and how they might see things differently based on the information about student work. In the case of Figure 2, the teacher would point out the missed criterion.

Student name: *Annie*

	Student	Teacher
Use different ways to represent ideas (e.g., numbers, pictures, words, diagrams, graphs)	✓	✓
Show all steps	✓	
Use mathematical symbols correctly	✓	✓
Use mathematical words from the math word wall when explaining	✓	✓
Show the steps you did (or your thinking) in order from first to last	✓	✓

Figure 2. Criteria-for-success form[1]. Note the difference in the student's and teacher's perception of which criteria have been met.

---

[1] adapted from A Guide to Descriptive Feedback. MISA London. London Region Professional Network, available at: https://youtu.be/PoFm5a6lWqM

Feedback becomes the tool for teachers and students to raise their consciousness, set specific goals supported by clarified next steps, and embrace the success that has been explicitly identified and planned for.

Chapter 7 / Giving Descriptive Feedback

WHAT THIS LOOKS LIKE IN YOUR SCHOOL

As an instructional leader you should:

1. Model what the descriptive feedback process looks like, beginning with the expected action, followed by the data of the present position and naming the gap in between, and ending with a discussion of how to close the gap and how you will support the teacher in doing so.

2. Seek to receive feedback as well, embracing the paradigm shift that invites reflection from every interaction.

3. Design and offer professional learning events for your faculty to learn how to provide descriptive feedback

4. Share articles with the faculty about the concept of descriptive feedback, such as:
   - Seven Keys to Effective Feedback by Grant Wiggins (2012)
   - Changing Classroom Practice by Dylan Wiliam (2007/2008)
   - The Secret to Effective Feedback, also by Dylan Wiliam (2016)

5. Teach your teachers about the intention of feedback and how to receive it, so they don't become defensive. It is not personal or a criticism.

6. Ask teachers to review student responses using Berger's, Rugen's & Woodfin's continuum of how students hear feedback (2014, p. 159) to foster conversation (*Table 1*).

> Doesn't see it as feedback for him/herself. Blames others. "That teacher is mean"
> ↓
> Hears feedback, but ignores. Does what he/she wants to do anyway.
> ↓
> Hears feedback, would like to revise, but doesn't know how.
> ↓
> Receives feedback, revises, successfully meets the goal.
> ↓
> Receives feedback, revises, successfully meets the goal, and can help others reach goal.

Table 1. Continuum of how students hear feedback
(from Berger, Rugen & Woodfin, 2014, p. 159)

7. Consider how often and when feedback should be given.

8. Choose priority points and the teacher's developmental needs to plan how much feedback should be offered at any one time. Link priority points to patterns of teacher and student data. Consider the context which is best suited for either oral or written feedback to make the right choice.

9. Reflect on how you can alter the master schedule and/or provide opportunities for teachers to work together honing their feedback capacity. Use the strategies below to make time for them to do that.

10. Watch the TED talk by Sheila Heen, a Harvard Law School professor, about how to help teachers use feedback to learn and grow and how to highlight the obstacles that get in the way[2].

---

[2] available at: https://www.youtube.com/watch?v=FQNbaKkYk_Q

Chapter 7 / Giving Descriptive Feedback

STRATEGIES TO TRY
PROVIDING DESCRIPTIVE FEEDBACK

1. As a department, team, or faculty, watch the video "A Group Critique Lesson" together[3]. Discuss how it would work with your students and the implications of this classroom practice for your planning and classroom culture.

2. As a department, team, or faculty, watch the video "Austin's Butterfly" together[4]. Discuss planning for your students to work together in feedback groups and the tools necessary for the students to gain skill in both giving and receiving feedback from each other. Discuss the implications of this classroom practice for your planning and classroom culture.

3. As a department, team, or faculty, watch the video "Steps of Descriptive Feedback: Success Criteria and Characteristics"[5]. Work on collaboratively planning success criteria for your next unit or lesson. Then share these criteria with students, and use them as the basis for providing descriptive feedback. Come back together as a group to discuss the effect of students receiving that feedback.

4. Practice using protocols as a team or department as you study student work and provide feedback together. Begin with the Collaborative Assessment Protocol, developed by Steve Seidel and his Project Zero colleagues at the Harvard Graduate School of Education[6], or the Tuning Protocol, developed by McDonald, Mohr, Dichter & McDonald (2007).

5. Discuss how you can make descriptive feedback a part of daily lessons and identify peer and self-assessment strategies which would support this process.

6. As a team or department, watch the video of John Hattie discussing what feedback looks like[7]. Consider how you would model these steps in your classroom.

7. Plan a training session for your students to gain the skills to be effective at giving peer-to-peer feedback. This doesn't happen by accident. Have them watch the "Austin's Butterfly" video and clarify behaviors. Have them practice the three dispositions: being kind, being specific, and being helpful.

8. Build a collection of exemplary student work that is reflective of common assessments. As a team, practice feedback skills using this work to build a common understanding and share experience.

9. Video feedback sessions and have the team watch them together to provide feedback on the feedback.

10. Never stop asking yourself the following questions: "How are we doing?"; "What's the evidence?"; and How can we improve?"

---

[3] available at: https://www.youtube.com/watch?v=_jixlo7kPx4
[4] available at: https://www.youtube.com/watch?v=PZo2PIhnmNY
[5] available at: https://www.youtube.com/watch?v=PoFm5a6lWqM
[6] available at: http://www.makinglearningvisibleresources.org/uploads/3/4/1/9/3419723/modified_collaborative_assessment_conference_protocol.pdf
[7] available at: https://www.youtube.com/watch?v=dvzeou_u2hM

BIBLIOGRAPHY

Bellon, J., Bellon, E., & Blank, M. A. (1992). *Teaching from a Research Knowledge Base: A Development and Renewal Process*. New York, NY: Macmillan Publishing Company.

Berger, R., Rugen, L., & Woodfin, L. (2014). *Leaders of Their Own Learning*. San Francisco, CA: Wiley and Sons.

Black, P., & Wiliam, D. (1998). Assessment and Classroom Learning. *Assessment in Education: Principles, Policy & Practice*, 5(1), 7-74. doi: 10.1080/0969595980050102

Davies, A. (2007). Making Classroom Assessment Work (2nd ed.). Courtenay, BC: Connections Publishing.

McDonald, J. P., Mohr, N., Dichter, A., & McDonald, E. C. (2007). *The Power of Protocols: An Educator's Guide to Better Practice* (2nd ed.). New York, NY: Teachers College Press.

Moss, C., & Brookhart, S. (2012). *Learning Targets: Helping Students Aim for Understanding in Today's Lesson*. Alexandria, VA: Association for Supervision and Curriculum Development.

Wiggins, G. (2012). Seven Keys to Effective Feedback. *Educational Leadership*, 70(1), 10–16.

Wiliam, D. (2007/2008). Changing Classroom Practice. *Educational Leadership*, 65(4), 36–42.

Wiliam, D. (2011). *Embedded Formative Assessment*. Bloomington, IN: Solution Tree Press.

Wiliam, D. (2016). The Secret of Effective Feedback. *Educational Leadership*, 73(7), 10–15.

Supporting Culturally Proficient Instruction and Learning Environments

INSTRUCTIONAL IMPLICATIONS
MOVING FROM DEPENDENCE TO INDEPENDENCE
CULTURALLY RESPONSIVE TEACHING

> *"Education either functions as an instrument which is used to facilitate integration of the younger generation into the logic of the present system and bring about conformity to it, or it becomes" the practice of freedom", the means by which men and women deal critically and creatively with reality and discover how to participate in the transformation of their world."*
>
> Richard Shaull in his foreword to Paulo Friere's *Pedagogy of the Oppressed* (2000, p. 34)

Building Your Instructional Leadership

As instructional leaders, we are always looking through a culturally proficient lens and ensuring that children come to a school where every classroom offers cultural proficiency to every child. As a result, it is important to facilitate professional learning, instructional practices, and a classroom environment that embodies cultural proficiency. This is how researchers Lindsey, Robins & Terrell define the concept of culture:

> "Everything you believe and everything you do that enables you to identify with people who are like you and that distinguishes you from people who differ from you... A culture is a group of people identified by shared history, values, and patterns of behavior." (Lindsey, Robins & Terrell, 2003, p. 41–42)

We see evidence of culture in many different areas, such as gender (hence the movie term "chick flicks" or going on a "girls' night out"), geographic origin ("the New York minute" or being viewed as a "Yankee" in the southern United States), our history and ancestry, language, occupation, physical characteristics, disabilities, race and ethnicity, sexual orientation, and shared interests, to name a few.

If we stop our journey toward cultural proficiency with this definition of culture, we might begin to stereotype and generalize, which could actually become dangerous and closed-minded. Instructional leaders encourage cultural proficiency instead. Cultural proficiency is defined as "...honoring the differences among cultures, viewing diversity as a benefit, and interacting knowledgeably and respectfully among a variety of cultural groups" (Lindsey, Roberts & Campbell Jones, 2005, p. 54). It is the concept of honoring that becomes paramount here. Instructional leaders model honoring and celebrating cultures represented in their school. Instructional leaders celebrate diversity as an enormous benefit and a great opportunity to expand perceptions, learn from each other, and become better as a result of this process. Culturally proficient people seek to understand what it is like to walk in the shoes of a diverse colleague, to wonder, question, and embrace dialogue as a way to learn and build an inclusive atmosphere. A culturally proficient school is a respectful and knowledgeable school. Shouldn't every school be described as knowledgeable and respectful?

The challenge for instructional leaders is how to build cultural proficiency among the faculty and how to communicate this proficiency to all of the students who attend your school.

Culturally proficient instructional leaders have their eyes and ears open at all times for cultural destructiveness (see Figure 1). They listen for comments like "Our scores would be great if we could just get rid of the ESL kids... special Ed kids... or... [just fill in the blank here]". Leaders are always listening for cultural incapacity as well and seek to address it. This usually falls into the category of low expectations for certain groups of students. This reminds me of a story a Latino colleague of mine shared about his nephew from Honduras who moved to a school in Maryland. Automatically he was placed into all of the lowest expectation courses the high school could offer. Fortunately for this student, his uncle was his advocate and had a high enough position in the school system to take on the school, the guidance counselor, and the schedule. He demanded that his nephew be placed in every advanced placement course even though his nephew had very limited English skills. In the end, not only did his nephew succeed, but he went on to be a Rhodes Scholar at Oxford University. What about all of the students who have been victims of low expectations without an advocate at their disposal?

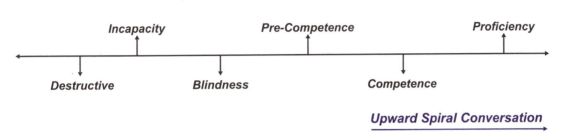

Figure 1. Cultural proficiency continuum (adapted from Lindsey, Robins & Terrell, 2003, p. 85)

A culturally proficient leader also addresses what some teachers actually strive for, which is cultural blindness. Some people believe that this is an honorable and fair position to take, the "I don't see color in my students. I treat all of my students the same." In fact, this communicates that personal heritage, culture, and background are not acknowledged or welcomed in this classroom, and individual needs will never be addressed. This is not the goal we strive for.

After an instructional leader addresses these negative approaches to diversity, teachers may move into the realm of cultural pre-competence. This means that there may be well-intended yet inappropriate comments, awkward ways of addressing differences, and potential insults and hurt feelings. Comments like "You're Latino. Can you be in charge of the Latino assembly?" is an example. The only way to become more comfortable is to be willing to be uncomfortable and continue to have conversations with each other. Ultimately, we become more culturally competent.

Instructional leader seeks to advocate changes in practice, policy, and procedures to provide equitable educational experiences for all students. They seek an ongoing education for themselves and their faculty. They celebrate diversity in the school as an opportunity for continuous learning and broadening of perspectives. This becomes the key to cultural proficiency, which is characterized by a clear sense of one's own culture, self-awareness, and knowledge of others.

INSTRUCTIONAL IMPLICATIONS

A school that doesn't embrace cultural proficiency makes way for educational inequity. A case in point is the failure to develop an academic identity in each and every student. Students who have not internalized academic identity for themselves tend to adopt the behaviors of academic dependence, and academic dependence leads to helplessness, and ultimately hopelessness.

Academic dependence in a student is not the same as deficiency. It suggests that teachers need to make an intentional effort to teach students the skills to become independent learners. We hope that independent learning, self-advocacy, and the creation of an academic identity happen by the third grade. The reality is that sometimes it doesn't happen by high school, and it may never happen, unless we all are intentional about addressing that goal.

At its extreme, academic dependence is the first leg of the "school-to-prison pipeline", to use the words of Zaretta Hammond (2015, p. 13) as she refers to the 2012 book by Michelle Alexander *The New Jim Crow: Mass Incarceration in the Age of Colorblindness* (2012) According to Hammond, research by the Southern Poverty Law Center suggests that teacher's instructional decisions result over time in students of color not receiving adequate literacy and content instruction, while being disproportionately disciplined for non-specific, subjective offenses such as defiance. As a result, these students end up spending valuable instructional time in the office rather than the classroom and can't keep up (Hammond, 2015, p. 13). Without social and emotional support, the downward spiral gains momentum that doesn't stop.

MOVING FROM DEPENDENCE TO INDEPENDENCE

Dependent learners need training in executive functioning, including the metacognition required to tackle a new project, breaking it down into and prioritizing the steps this process should take, diagnosing what scaffolding is needed, and using strategies and processes for tackling a new task. Moving to independence means studying and practicing Costa & Kallick's habits of mind (2009) to get unstuck. Some of these habits are using all of your resources, practicing perseverance, and embracing active engagement, such as problem solving with a peer, which puts information into long-term memory. These activities support an academically rich experience. The opposite is what Martin Haberman (1991) calls "the pedagogy of poverty", the pedagogy of rote recall and lecture-based teaching.

CULTURALLY RESPONSIVE TEACHING

Zaretta Hammond defines culturally responsive teaching as "...an educator's ability to recognize students' cultural displays of learning and meaning making and [the ability to] respond [to these cultural displays] positively and constructively with teaching moves that use cultural knowledge as a scaffold to connect what the student knows to new concepts and content in order to promote effective information processing. "All the while," she continues "the educator understands the importance of being in relationship and having social-emotional connection to the student in order to create a safe space for learning" (2015, p. 15).

This social-emotional connection is a must to enhance learning and make students feel safe, hopeful of success, and willing to take on the challenge of learning (Tatum, 2009).

The ultimate goal of culturally responsive teaching is for every student to become ready for rigor and independent learning. This means that instructional leaders train themselves and their faculty to:

1. *become aware* of cultural archetypes, socio-political context around race and language, recognize their own brain triggers around race and culture, broaden perspectives of culturally and linguistically diverse learning behaviors;

2. *create learning partnerships*, beginning with the teacher and student, diminish stereotype threat and micro-aggressions, and strike the balance between push and support (become so called "warm demanders");

3. *build intellectual capacity* (mental muscle) through appropriate challenge, culturally relevant examples and materials, cognitive routines, teaching metacognition, and formative assessments as learning methods and means of reflection; and

4. *create a learning environment* which is intellectually and socially safe to take risks, the one that encourages student voice and choice, student agency, a sense of control in the classroom, and a sense of hope and optimism for learning by offering structured tasks for independent success and restorative justice to manage conflicts (Hammond, 2015).

Every culture brings with it the blessing of deep roots. Culturally proficient educators and (international) schools fostering global-mindedness know this is true. What does culture have to do with it? Everything. Color-blindness is not a virtue.

Unfortunately, many schools just scratch the surface. I call it the three "F"s: food, flags, and festivals. You may have seen this; someone proposes "Let's have a global night event", and everyone comes wearing their favorite country costume, brings a favorite dish, and waves flags. But cultural proficiency remains where it was before, if proficiency is the right term. Ideally, we move from the surface (putting your toe in the ocean) to the shallows (now our foot is in the shallow end). A shallow-level conversation means that we might have a discussion about varying concepts of time, rules about eye contact, personal space, attitudes toward the elders, or appropriate touching. The ultimate goal is to move our conversation to a place of deep understanding, which means that we dig into the depth of our respective cultures. This begins with a conversation about our knowledge and unconscious assumptions that govern our worldview and guide our sense of ethics, spirituality, health, cooperation, or competition. As Jawaharlal Nehru, the first Prime Minister of India said: "Culture is the widening of the mind and of the spirit."

Building Your Instructional Leadership

WHAT THIS LOOKS LIKE IN YOUR SCHOOL

As an instructional leader you should:

1. ask yourself how your school addresses the needs of low-performing students of color.
2. ask yourself how you support struggling students to become independent learners.
3. ask yourself how you and your colleagues have operationalized the principles of culturally responsive teaching.
4. consider when and how you can ask this question: "Will you tell me your story? I would like to know how you came to this point of view?"
5. consider who you are in relation to the person you're leading.
6. recognize and assess how your culture affects the culture of others.
7. describe how your culture relates to how you lead your faculty.
8. think about how the culture of your school affects those with other cultures.
9. identify the cultural norms of your school/school system. What are their manifestations?
10. reflect on how you invite various voices to the table for diverse conversations.

Chapter 8 / Supporting Culturally Proficient Instruction and Learning Environments

STRATEGIES TO DEVELOP CULTURAL PROFICIENCY

1. Watch the CBS video "Harlem Children's Zone"[1]. What are the key ideas? What implications do those ideas have for your classroom?

2. Read the quotations below and circle the one that connects most with your thinking. Share the quote you selected with your team or department and why it resonates with you.

   "The longer we listen to one another with real attention, the more commonality we will find in all our lives. That is, if we are careful to exchange with one another life stories and not simply opinions. " Barbara Deming (U. S. author and activist, 1917–)

   "Normal is in the eye of the beholder." Whoopi Goldberg (U. S. actress, 1955–)

   "Sometimes I feel discriminated against, but it does not make me angry. It merely astonishes me. How can they deny themselves the pleasure of my company? It's beyond me." Zora Neale Hurston (U. S. writer, 1903–1960)

   "If we are to achieve a richer culture, rich in contrasting values, we must recognize the whole gamut of human potentialities and so weave a less arbitrary social fabric, one in which each diverse human gift will find a fitting place." Margaret Mead (US anthropologist, 1901–1978)

3. As a team, discuss the four stages (or steps) of cultural competence (awareness, curiosity, learning, and participation)[2]. Start by asking the following questions:

   What are you aware of?
   What are you curious about?
   What do you want to learn?
   With whom do you need to participate?

4. Using the "Cognitive Rigor Matrix, analyze your lesson plans for the week to come. Where do you see the presence of rigor as defined by the matrix? How can you raise the level of rigor assessed?

---

[1] available at: https://www.youtube.com/watch?v=Dio-xN6xc_w
[2] also see Dr. Craig's video at: https://www.youtube.com/watch?v=mwsegcMsolY

	Recall and reproduction	Basic application of skills and concepts	Strategic thinking and reasoning	Extended thinking
Remember	Recall or locate basic facts, details, events.	N/A	N/A	N/A
Understand	Describe or explain who, what, where, when, or how.	Explain relationships, summarize, identify main ideas.	Explain generalize, or connect ideas using supporting evidence.	Explain how concepts or ideas specifically relate to other content domains.
Apply	Use a language structure or word relationships to determine meaning.	Obtain and interpret information using text features.	Apply a concept in a new context.	Select or devise an approach among many alternatives to research a novel problem.
Analyze	Identify whether information is contained in a graph, table, and so on.	Distinguish between relevant and irrelevant information.	Analyze interrelationships among concepts, issues, or problems.	Analyze complex or abstract themes or perspectives.
Evaluate	N/A	N/A	Justify or critique conclusions drawn.	Apply understanding in a novel way, with justification.
Create	Brainstorm ideas about topic.	Generate hypothesis based on observation or prior knowledge.	Develop a complex model for a given situation.	Articulate a new voice, new knowledge, or perspective.

Table 1. Cognitive rigor matrix with sample tasks
Adapted from Karin K. Hess' Cognitive Rigor Matrix (2009)

5. Take the 12-item GRIT scale by Duckworth et al. (2007)[3] and see where you fall in the area of perseverance. Have your students do the same. Discuss what not giving up, hard work, and perseverance look like in your classroom.

6. Examine your own cultural identity. We must first understand ourselves as cultural beings before we can understand anyone else's. Use the All-About-Me graphic organizer to assist you.

7. Map your own cultural reference points: How do your family members identify themselves ethnically and racially? Where did you live? What family folklore or stories did you hear growing up? What are some of your family traditions?

---

[3] available at: http://www.sas.upenn.edu/~duckwort/images/12-item%20Grit%20Scale.05312011.pdf

8. Practice using the Mindful Reflection Protocol by Dray & Wisneski (2011)[4] in your classroom. Share the results with your colleagues and discuss next steps.

9. Investigate the Teaching Tolerance[5] website for activities to use with your students to broaden perspectives such as Graça Machel or Using Editorial Cartoons to teach Social Justice.

10. Explore the MindsetWorks website[6] presenting Carol Dweck's research on growth mindset (2006) and how all students can learn to get smarter with effective effort.

---

4   available at: http://ready4rigor.com/wp-content/uploads/2015/02/Protocol-for-Checking-Unconscious-Bias.pdf
5   available at: http://www.tolerance.org/activities
6   available at: https://www.mindsetworks.com/programs/brainology-for-schools

BIBLIOGRAPHY

Alexander, M. (2012). *The New Jim Crow: Mass Incarceration in the Age of Colorblindness*. New York, NY: The New Press.

Costa, A., & Kallick, B. (Eds.) (2009). *Learning and Leading with Habits of Mind: 16 Essential Characteristics for Success*. Alexandria, VA: Association for Supervision and Curriculum Development.

Dray, B. J. & Wisneski, D. B. (2011). Mindful Reflection as a Process for Developing Culturally Responsive Practices. *TEACHING Exceptional Children*, 44(1), 28–36.

Duckworth, A.L., Peterson, C., Matthews, M.D., & Kelly, D.R. (2007). Grit: Perseverance and passion for long-term goals. Journal of Personality and Social Psychology, 92(6), 1087–1101.

Dweck, C. S. (2006). *Mindset: The New Psychology of Success*. New York, NY: Random House.

Friere, P. (2000). *Pedagogy of the Oppressed* (30th anniversary ed., M. B. Ramos, Trans.). New York, NY: Bloomsbury. (Original work published 1968)

Haberman, M. (1991). The Pedagogy of Poverty Versus Good Teaching. *Phi Delta Kappan*, 73(4), 290–294.

Hammond, Z. (2015). *Culturally Responsive Teaching and the Brain: Promoting Authentic Engagement and Rigor Among Culturally and Linguistically Diverse Students*. Thousand Oaks, CA: Corwin Press.

Hess, K. K., Carlock, D., Jones, B., & Walkup, J. W. (2009). *What Exactly Do "Fewer, Clearer, and Higher Standards" Really Look Like in the Classroom? Using a Cognitive Rigor Matrix to Analyze Curriculum, Plan Lessons, and Implement Assessments*. Dover, NH: National Center for Assessment. Retrieved from http://schools.nyc.gov/NR/rdonlyres/D106125F-FFF0-420E-86D9-254761638C6F/0/HessArticle.pdf.

Lindsey, D., Martinez, R. and Lindsey, R. Culturally Proficient Coaching: Supporting Educators to Create Equitable Schools. Corwin Press. Thousand Oaks, CA. 2007.

Lindsey, R. B., Roberts, L. M., & Campbell Jones, F. (2005). The Culturally Proficient School: An Implementation Guide for School Leaders. Thousand Oaks, CA: Corwin Press.

Lindsey, R. B., Robins, K. N., & Terrell, R. D. (2003). *Cultural Proficiency: A Manual for School Leaders* (2nd ed.). Thousand Oaks, CA: Corwin Press.

Sousa, D. (2011). *How the Brain Learns.* Thousand Oaks, CA: Corwin Press.

Tatum, B. D. (2009). Teaching White Students About Racism: The Search for White Allies and the Restoration of Hope. In *Foundations of Critical Race Theory in Education* (pp. 277-288). New York, NY: Routledge.

Tatum, B. D. (2003). Why Are All the Black Kids Sitting Together in the Cafeteria? And Other Conversations About Race (5th anniversary edition). New York, NY: Basic Books.

Observing for Learning

LOOKING FOR LEARNING

SIX INSTRUCTIONAL CATEGORIES WHICH SUPORT HIGH-LEVEL LEARNING

NOTE-TAKING TECHNIQUES

ORGANIZING DATA INTO CLAIMS, EVIDENCE, AND IMPACT ON STUDENT LEARNING

> *I believe in evidence. I believe in observation, measurement, and reasoning, confirmed by independent observers. I'll believe anything, no matter how wild and ridiculous, if there is evidence for it. The wilder and more ridiculous something is, however, the firmer and more solid the evidence will have to be.*
>
> Isaac Asimov,
> *The Roving Mind* (1983)

In every US state teachers must be observed in a formal and documented process. Most independent schools have embraced the same requirement and have developed their own professional growth and evaluation systems. These may vary in performance standards and how often a teacher is observed and by whom, but observation is a constant. The bigger question is how can instructional leaders make observation a learning opportunity for both the observer and the teacher. How can instructional leaders reframe the observation process to be one of a dialogue, as opposed to them versus us? In so many cases the formal observation process has been reduced to a game, a dog-and-pony show that doesn't really capture what is going on in a classroom.

I would like to share four anecdotes from my own experience to make a point. In the first, Pete, a high school English teacher, very proudly invited me to his classroom to behold his perfectly written mastery objective on the board. "Isn't this great Fran? Beautifully written, right?". "Yes," I replied, waiting for the punchline. "Well Fran, this same objective has been written here for the past two months. My administrator has been in and out, checking off that I do indeed have a mastery objective written, so hurray for me. It is the same objective, and he doesn't even know the difference. His hoop jumping is a farce."

Anecdote number two takes place in a middle school science lab class. I was jointly observing with the principal, comparing our observations at the end. The teacher was doing everything right; the room was set up beautifully beforehand not to waste instructional time getting materials, and all of the students were highly engaged in a hands-on experiment. They seemed to know what to do and were busy going through the motions. But there was something odd about it. The teacher was moving from group to group as expected, but there was no informal interchange. There was no dialogue between the teacher and the students other than "everything good here?" and "you're all okay?" And what became clear as day was that the teacher never called a single student by their first name, and not a single personal remark was shared between the teacher and any of his students. It was April. When was he planning on learning his students' names?

The third anecdote takes place in a fourth grade class that a principal asked me to observe with her. She picked this teacher because she was so proud of his teaching and was sure that I would be equally impressed. As we entered the classroom, I thought that it was an art lesson in mixing white and black paint for the perfect shade of gray. I wasn't sure. The gray was to be painted on rectangular pieces of paper to be taped around the doorways in the room. I began interviewing the students: "Why are you doing this?", "What is that activity teaching you to notice?", "What is the purpose of this lesson?" Not a single student could answer any of the questions. However, they were quick to tell me how much they loved their teacher, how much fun the class was, and how well organized he was. Indeed, there was a very warm rapport, and the materials were perfectly arranged. After much probing, it turned out that this ambiguous lesson was a social studies lesson in support of a standard which required the students to name and identify five major architectural achievements from Ancient Rome. This activity was supposed to clarify the creation of the archway. The students did not know that.

The last anecdote takes place in a high school math class. All the students were wildly enthusiastic, and whenever the teacher posed a question to the students, every hand shot up in the air with great energy. Yet only the four same students were called on for responses every time. When I interviewed the students afterwards, they let me in on the game. Whenever an observer was in the classroom, they were trained to raise hands when the teacher asked a question. If they knew the answer, they'd raise the left hand. If they were clueless, they'd raise the right hand. The sum total picture looked like active engagement and enthusiasm for an untrained eye, whereas only four students knew the answers.

LOOKING FOR LEARNING

I have many more anecdotes to share, but they all point to the lack of reliability and validity of formal observation when the focus is on the teacher and what the teacher says and does, as opposed to the students and what evidence they can provide of their learning. This beats the purpose of any observation, which is to assess the level of students' learning.

And the purpose of this chapter is to highlight an observational paradigm shift from a checklist of teacher moves to evidence of student mastery, because the two may or may not correlate. Instructional leaders need to interview students and seek evidence of their understanding of the learning target. Students need to be able to discuss what they are doing and why. They should be able to highlight what their content and skill struggles are. Questions that an instructional leader poses to students should serve to find evidence of learning. Here are some (*Table 1*):

> **Is there any learning going on?**
> What are you learning today? (knowledge).
> What are you learning about? (skill/understanding).
> Why do you think you are learning this?
> Tell me something you are learning.
> Is this new learning?
> Are you practicing something you already learned? (skill/consolidation).
> Can you tell me how this is connected to what you have learned before,
> What you already knew or could do?
>
> **Is the learning appropriate?**
> What did you know about this before?
> What do you know now that you didn't know before? Why?
> Is this learning too easy? Too hard? Just right?
> Is this difficult to learn?
>
> **Is the learning sufficient?**
> Is the learning challenging?
> What do you think you did well? What was the hardest?
> What did you enjoy about learning this?
> Do you enjoy learning this? Why?
> What's been most exciting about this learning?
> How do you know how successful you are in learning this?
> How long have you been doing this?
> How long have you been doing this?
> What will you be learning next?
>
> **How is the context helping or hindering the learning?**
> What helps you to learn?
> What stops your learning?
> What do you do if you are stuck with your learning?
> Is this classroom a safe place to learn?
> Do you have any choices in your learning?

Table 1. Looking for learning questions (adopted from the Looking for Learning program developed by Fieldwork Education; London, UK[1])

Instructional leaders intentionally shift focus from the teacher to the student. *Table 2* shows the differences between the two.

---

[1] for more information visit: http://www.greatlearning.com/lfl/

Teacher-focused principal: Lesson plans are complete and meet district expectations. Teacher plans for low-, medium-, and high-level students.
Student-focused principal: Student work/outcomes look much the same regardless of students' achievement level.
Teacher-focused principal: The teacher is moving around and seems to have a great rapport with students.
Student-focused principal: Although the teacher is mobile, four students have worked three of the first set of problems incorrectly.
Teacher-focused principal: Students are well behaved and seem to be engaged in the content.
Student-focused principal: Students are working independently. Two students have put away their unfinished work and are reading a novel. One student is doodling on his notebook. The teacher provides low-level feedback such as "Good job" and "You're working hard."
Teacher-focused principal: The learning goal is posted in the front of the class.
Student-focused principal: Only two of eight students chosen at random could recall the learning goal and only one student could demonstrate it with mastery.
Teacher-focused principal: Students are answering questions correctly and seem to have mastered the goal.
Student-focused principal: Each time the teacher asked questions, the same three students correctly answered them.

Table 2. When we shift our focus from observing the teacher to observing the students (source unknown)

SIX INSTRUCTIONAL CATEGORIES WHICH SUPORT HIGH-LEVEL LEARNING

Charlotte Danielson (1996), Robert Marzano (2013), Kim Marshall (2001), and James Stronge (2003, 2013) have all written books and designed observation documents, rubrics, and matrices which provide the language of expert instruction for instructional leaders to follow. A skilled instructional leader and observer knows that their skill does not depend on any one program. Expertise is not tied to the number of observable indicators you can check off or your reliability as a rater based on correct answers to your organizational practice videos. Rather, a skilled instructional leader and observer knows that there are some areas of skill that need to be present in any lesson, any grade level, any content area on any day, regardless of the program that a school or school system has adopted. These skill areas include:

Clarity of instructional purpose and accuracy of content

An instructional leader will speak with teachers about whether their planning documents (learning targets, activities to master the learning targets, accuracy of the content, higher-level thinking questions that guide students to conceptual understanding of the content, warm-ups, and extended field work assignments, aka homework) directly align to the skills and concepts highlighted in the lesson. Then she or he will reflect on the success of the lesson based on the evidence of student work and thinking. Much of this evidence she or he will gather from interviews with the students.

Psychologically safe, supportive, and challenging learning environment

An instructional leader will observe whether the students are taking risks, reflecting on their mistakes, and receiving teacher's support and enthusiasm for taking these risks. As an observer, she or he will note evidence of rigor, coupled with support and acknowledgement of perseverance when tasks are difficult, paying particular attention to respect and appreciation for not giving up, for using different strategies, and making effective effort (Dweck, 2006). She or he will observe if the classroom has the atmosphere of fairness and differentiated support, and if the teacher is seeking students' feedback on how she or he can best support their learning. The observer will note if the students are greeted at the door, called by name with appropriate pronunciation, and whether the interchange about the content is accompanied by a relationship-building dialogue.

Classroom control, structure, and management

An instructional leader/observer will look for both implementation and use of routines, procedures, and self-assessment of student behavior in classrooms. Established norms, rules of conduct, and self and group reflection on these norms and rules should be a regular thing. Safety procedures should be followed, as should the efficient time-management procedures for maximizing instructional time (e.g., handing out and collecting materials, entering and exiting the classroom, or reviewing work).

Intellectual engagement

In the classroom, an instructional leader/observer will seek evidence of intellectual rigor, encouragement of higher-level thinking, and the cultures of thinking (Ritchhart, 2015). The observer should see if the habits of mind (Costa & Kallick, 2009) such as questioning, problem posing, perseverance, making decisions given incomplete information, and cognitive debate have been planned for. The observer should notice if the students transform content into different forms. The observer should also note whether they are engaged in activities that challenge thinking, have alternative points of view, require different possible solutions, and rely on rigorous thinking in their conclusions.

Mastery of learning by all students

An instructional leader/observer will check whether the teacher consistently collects evidence of student learning. Formative assessments should be planned for and embedded throughout the lesson, and both the teacher and the students should be "looking for the proof of learning" in anticipation of learning gaps and next steps in teaching and support. The teacher should be giving descriptive feedback to the students and modify the lesson based on the collected information, whereas the students should set goals and action steps based on their findings about their work against the set criteria and exemplars. The teacher should adjust support and resources to enable each and every students to master the content and skills.

Professionalism

I was once observing a teacher who was replying to emails for fourteen minutes while the students were waiting patiently for her to turn around, and one other time, the same teacher returned to the classroom from lunch eight minutes after the bell rang. What I mean under professionalism here is that the teacher is prepared, present, and ready to start the class on time. And while these properties of professionalism are not often the object of observer's scrutiny in the classroom, it manifests itself through collaboration at team and department meetings, through the sharing of resources and documents, and through investment in the teaching success of colleagues.

NOTE-TAKING TECHNIQUES

Oftentimes, instructional leaders will note down evidence of student response to the five or six instructional categories listed above. The notes will include the questions posed, so that the teacher and the observer can analyze the level of rigor embedded in teacher's questions (recall? analysis?), the number of wait seconds between the question and students' response, the type of relationship-building comments or sarcastic comments that might crop up, or the kind of questions the students ask (confusion? need for clarity? intellectual debate?). In addition, the notes can be organized in different categories, such as those that track time or frequency of activities:

Time notes
- how long did the warm-up take;
- how long did the transition between activities take;
- how long did the teacher-centered lecture take before any checking for understanding;
- how long did an activity take and if it was reasonable;
- for how long were the students engaged or off task.

Frequency notes
- how many students participated in the class;
- how many students were confused;
- how many students knew the purpose of the lesson;
- how many students were late, absent, sharpening pencils, getting the bathroom pass;
- how many students showed proof of their own mastery.

ORGANIZING DATA INTO CLAIMS, EVIDENCE, AND IMPACT ON STUDENT LEARNING

Lastly, observations can be organized into categories based on recurring trends and patterns. Observers can match these trends and patterns to their evaluation instrument. For example, the trend of warm and welcome comments to students throughout the lesson could be assessed as strength in the category of positive learning environment. If the students are confused about the purpose of the lesson or can't understand and complete a task, the observer could assess it as a problem in the clarity of instruction.

It is these patterns and trends, supported by the evidence collected by the observer, that make the observation report as the point of reference for the post-observation conference between the teacher and observer. What is ultimately being assessed in this dialogue is how the above trends affect students and their learning. In a postobservation conference, a skilled instructional leader will stick to the data and steer the discussion toward identifying the next steps the teacher can take based on the impact on student learning. To quote Dylan Wiliam, "If we create a culture where every teacher believes they need to improve, not because they are not good enough but because they can be even better, there is no limit to what we can achieve."

Chapter 9 / Observing for Learning

WHAT THIS LOOKS LIKE IN YOUR SCHOOL

As an instructional leader you should:

1. share, discuss, and adopt a professional growth and evaluation document with the faculty, fostering a "no secrets" school.

2. provide instruction and support for the teachers in what each of the standards, domains, or indicators mean in a classroom, so that teachers can be successful.

3. discuss what looking for learning looks and sounds like with the faculty.

4. take teachers on "looking for learning" scavenger hunts through the school and discuss patterns and trends with them.

5. take notes during observation and share them with the teachers at postobservation conferences[2].

6. seek to collect additional information from walkthroughs, informal visits, interviews with students, and analysis of student work to increase the reliability and validity of teaching and learning trends in each classroom. Hone your observation skills by using an observation form like the one in *Table 3*.

	Exemplary	Meets expectation	Approaching expectation	Not meeting expectation	Not applicable
Learning targets: The daily learning target is connected to a supporting learning target. Students discuss the target at the beginning of the lesson, during, and at the end (with debrief).					Note why practice was skipped.
Do now: A short assignment relevant to course learning targets get kids on task. Students can handle the work independently and produce tangible evidence of understanding.					Note why practice was skipped.
Divided practice: Teachers gradually release responsibility, creating a safe space for students to practice the task with support, and give students experience with success.					Note why practice was skipped.
Catch and release as needed: Teacher "catches" students by class together to check on progress, share strategies, common misunderstanding, or address frequent actions or issues.					Note why practice was skipped.

Table 3. Sample observation checklist
(adapted from Berger, Rugen & Woodfin, 2014)

---

[2] you can make good use of the Instructional conversation protocol (tool 4.3), designed by Killion et al. (2012), which is also available at https://learningforward.org/docs/coachingmatters/killiontoolch4-4.pdf

Building Your Instructional Leadership

7. make and discuss an analysis of team-wide or departmental patterns and trends in teaching and learning with the team of teachers who generated the data. One way to do that is to ask the team to make a "gap-analysis"[3].

8. arrange for teachers to observe each other following a data-driven protocol and analyze their own peer-observation data[4].

9. facilitate the creation of next steps for continual pedagogical growth, based on the analysis of data by the teachers themselves.

10. ask teachers to design professional growth goals and actions plans for the next week based on the post-observation conference.

---

[3] you can make a good use of the tool 8.3, see footnote above
[4] you can make a good use of tool 4.5, see footnotes above

STRATEGIES TO OBSERVE CLASSROOM INSTRUCTION

Who made up the rule that only administrators can observe teachers? By design, this sets up a you-versus-us mentality, a structure by which the principal holds all of the cards, and which damages trust and psychological safety between the teacher and the administrators. The following strategies help the instructional leader to distribute leadership through collaboration, collaborative observation, learning from each other, video recording, and reflective practice initiated by the teacher. The sum total of all of these behaviors is the power to shift conversation, raise the level of ownership and pedagogical skills among the faculty, and expand instructional leadership throughout the school.

1. Have the team or department watch "Katie Banyon's Lesson: Expert Analysis". Highlight and critique the lesson. Compare how your critique correlates with the one that Katie received. Read Katie's response to the critique[5].

2. Arrange for teams/departments to go on learning walks together. Observe one beforehand in the video "Learning Walks"[6]. Discuss what the benefits are of doing observations together.

3. Using the instructional expertise of your team, practice "Free-Up Fridays"[7] to share instructional expertise. Watch this video as a model and use instructional expertise agenda[8] (instructional expertise facilitators' guide) to do that.

4. Make learning public (teaching and learning being observed by other teachers) through teacher time-outs to visit each other[9].

5. Create an inquiry team in your school[10]. Watch the video[11] together, review the handbook as a model, and discuss how an inquiry team might benefit instruction for the faculty and students in your school.

6. Watch Kathleen Cushman's video on "Teaching as a Team Sport"[12]. How does your school culture currently support this idea? How can you embrace the paradigm of expanding our instructional skill through this process?

7. Use video recording to improve your own practice. Record and reflect upon your teaching practice and how it aligns with your school's teaching and learning framework. Guide your reflection with your administrator. Watch these videos to learn how[13].

---

5   available at: https://www.teachingchannel.org/videos/reading-lesson-plan-critique
6   available at: https://www.teachingchannel.org/videos/the-learning-walk
7   available at: https://www.teachingchannel.org/videos/share-instructional-expertise
8   available at: https://www.teachingchannel.org/instructional-expertise-module-sac
9   available at: https://www.teachingchannel.org/videos/teacher-time-out
10   make use of the Inquiry team handbook available at: https://dsovton1574d2.cloudfront.net/resources/document/resource/13954/Inquiry Team Handbook_2008.PDF
11   available at: https://www.teachingchannel.org/videos/inquiry-protocol-nvps
12   available at: https://www.teachingchannel.org/videos/coaching-for-teachers-and-students-nvps
13   https://www.teachingchannel.org/videos/improve-teaching-with-video; https://www.teachingchannel.org/videos/use-video-to-improve-teaching-ousd

8. Record a lesson and review it in the privacy of your home. Discuss your revelations with a colleague. Learn tips for recording video in your classroom[14].

9. Read "How to Give Professional Feedback" by Susan M. Brookhart and Connie M. Moss (2015). Solicit feedback from teachers to improve your feedback.

10. Have teachers collect feedback from students to reflect and improve their practice[15]. Share your findings at a post-observation conference including next steps.

---

14 available at: https://www.teachingchannel.org/videos/videotaping-tips-for-teachers
15 make use of the video available at: https://www.teachingchannel.org/videos/improve-teaching-with-studentfeedback

BIBLIOGRAPHY

Asimov, A. (1983). *The Roving Mind*. Buffalo, NY: Prometheus Books.

Berger, R., Rugen, L., & Woodfin, L. (2014). *Leaders of Their Own Learning*. San Francisco, CA: Wiley and Sons.

Brookhart, S. M., & Moss, C. M. (2015). How to Give Professional Feedback. *Educational Leadership*, 72(7), 24–30.

Costa, A., & Kallick, B. (Eds.) (2009). *Learning and Leading with Habits of Mind: 16 Essential Characteristics for Success*. Alexandria, VA: Association for Supervision and Curriculum Development.

Danielson, C. (1996). *Enhancing Professional Practice: A Framework for Teaching*. Alexandria, VA: Association for Supervision and Curriculum Development.

Dweck, C. S. (2006). *Mindset: The New Psychology of Success*. New York, NY: Random House.

Killion, J., Harrison, C., Bryan, C., & Clifton, H. (2012). *Coaching matters*. Oxford, OH: Learning Forward.

Marshall, K. (2001). *Rethinking Teacher Supervision and Evaluation: How to Work Smart, Build Collaboration, and Close the Achievement Gap* (2nd ed.). San Francisco, CA: Jossey-Bass.

Marzano, R., & Toth, M. (2013). *Teacher Evaluation That Makes a Difference: A New Model for Teacher Growth and Student Achievement*. Alexandria, VA: Association for Supervision and Curriculum Development.

Ritchhart, R. (2015). *Creating Cultures of Thinking: The 8 Forces We Must Master to Truly Transform Our Schools*. San Francisco, CA: Jossey-Bass.

Stronge, J. H. (2013). *Evaluating What Good Teachers Do: Eight Research-Based Standards for Assessing Teacher Excellence*. New York, NY: Routledge.

Stronge, J. H., & Tucker, P. (2003). *Handbook on Teacher Evaluation*. Larchmont, NY: Eye on Education.

Coaching Conversations

GOALS AND BENEFITS OF COACHING

PRINCIPAL AS THE FORMATIVE COACH

COACHING SKILLS

WHAT DATA TO COLLECT TO SUPPORT COACHING CONVERSATIONS

GROWTH MODEL

COACHING CONVERSATIONS

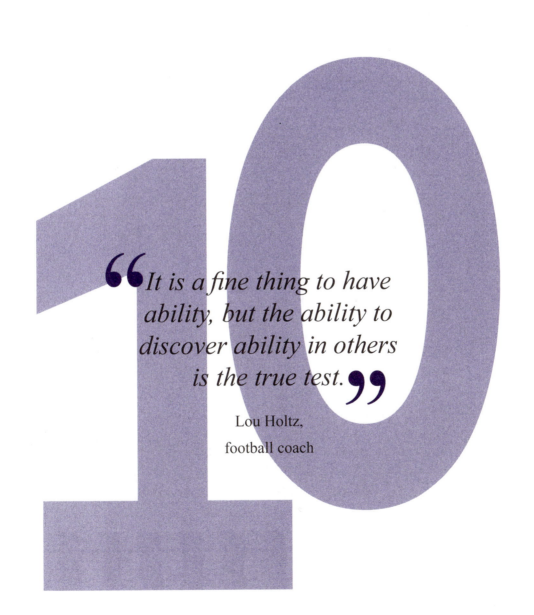

> *"It is a fine thing to have ability, but the ability to discover ability in others is the true test."*
>
> Lou Holtz,
> football coach

Whatever its form, coaching is a partnership that fosters reflection and modification. Ideally, a change or a transformation occurs by virtue of the coaching experience. Andre Gawande (2011) captures the complexities of this partnership as follows: "The concept of a coach is slippery. Coaches are not teachers, but they teach. They're not your boss—in professional tennis, golf and skating, the athlete hires and fires the coach—but they can be bossy. They don't even have to be good at the sport. The famous Olympic gymnastics coach Bela Karolyi couldn't do a split if his life depended on it. Mainly they observe, they judge, and they guide."

GOALS AND BENEFITS OF COACHING

Ultimately, instructional leaders seek to point their teachers toward best practices they can add to their repertoire. They wear the hat of instructional coach when they show teachers what good teaching looks like by taking them to the classes of master teachers and by analyzing videos of effective teacher performance. Instructional leaders want to encourage teachers to take risks and experiment with new strategies and practices without being totally sure of the outcome.

The research of Bruce Joyce and Beverly Showers (2002) showed that attaining these goals makes a great difference, as coached teachers and principals practiced new strategies more often and with more skill than those who were not coached. They also found that coached teachers better incorporated these new learning strategies in their lessons, had greater long-term retention of their learning and skills, and were much more likely to explain the purposes and uses of new strategies and skills (p. 86–87). Furthermore, Jim Knight found in his research (2007) that when teachers receive support for professional learning, 90% of the teachers embrace and implement new learning (p. 4). Biancarosa, Bryk & Dexter (2010) and Vanderburg & Stephens (2010) found significant student achievement in students whose teachers received consistent coaching. "The beliefs and practices of coached teachers became more consistent with best practices as defined by national and state standards", report Vanderburg and Stephens (2010).

PRINCIPAL AS THE FORMATIVE COACH

Principals are the primary instructional leaders in their schools. As a result, they are also coaches of every teacher as well as of every instructional, literacy, or math coach who reports to them. It is the principal's job to share their vision with those coaches and teachers, guide their work, set expectations, review their progress, and build coaching partnership. Formative coaching begins with looking at students' work and showing what deep analysis of teaching and learning looks and sounds like. Deep analysis informs the next steps that instructional coaches need to take (Nidus & Sadder, 2011).

As a formative coach, the principal finds ways to weave student work and the analysis data into every conversation and uses these conversations as a way for instructional coaches to focus on the faculty. *Table 1* highlights the opportunities that instructional leaders can take advantage of to foster these deep, data-driven conversations about teaching and learning.

1. Focus on student work during your classroom observations and follow-up conversations.
2. Encourage teachers to create student work portfolios.
3. Talk with teachers about the student work they post on bulletin boards.
4. Use student work to inform meetings about student behavior plans or any teacher discussions of students who need social or behavior interventions.
5. Build in time for teachers to discuss student work in grade-level teams as well as across grade levels.
6. Develop a shared language of assessment and performance standards.
7. Always have teachers bring student work to professional development activities to serve as a basis for discussion.
8. Choose one kind of student work—for example, writing genres or graphic organizers—to focus on as a school community.
9. Display and discuss various kinds of data that teachers collect.
10. Encourage teachers to send student work folders to next year's teacher.

Table 1. Ten ways to weave student work into the fabric of your school
(adopted from Nidus & Sadder, 2011)

COACHING SKILLS

Effective coaches (formative, instructional, literacy, mathematics, or cognitive, to name a few) model relationship building and asking the right questions, so that teachers can reflect on their instructional choices and expand their pedagogy for the benefit of students.

Relationship building

Coaching begins with building trust and emotional connection with the teachers. We discussed in depth the importance of relationship building through psychological safety, empathy, trust, and collaboration in Section 1 of this book. A psychologically safe (confidential, non-judgmental) relationship encourages dialogue and discussion. Classroom observations, working side by side, and discussion about issues in practice build on the trusting relationship which has been created.

Providing feedback

The next step in this coaching partnership is providing descriptive, data-driven feedback based on the classroom observations and interactions between the coach and the teacher or her/his students. The critical attributes of descriptive feedback and strategies to provide feedback are highlighted in Chapter 7. Based on the feedback provided, the coach offers a variety of research-based practices and strategies for the teacher to choose from as their next steps for learning and growing in their pedagogy.

Asking invitational questions

A critical skill every coach must learn and implement is how to ask questions that will foster reflection and dialogue with the teacher. Here are some examples of how to ask invitational questions:

- Use plural forms: "What are reasons for...? What strategies are you...?";
- Use exploratory/tentative language: "What might your thoughts be about...? What are some of the possibilities...? What are yor hunches about...?";
- Make positive assumptions: "As you examine the data, what are some of the patterns emerging? What might be your indicators that the teacher is developing?";
- Leave questions open-ended, so that they can't be answered with yes/no or one word: "What was your thinking about... (versus "Have you thought about").

Many coaches find sentence stems helpful as they are learning the skill of asking questions to stimulate teacher's thinking, reflection, and modification (Table 2).

Active listening stems	Non-judgmental responses
• So... • In other words... • What you are saying is... Is that correct? Am I missing anything? • You are saying many things... • Is there anything else you feel I should know?	• I noticed how when you...the students really... (to identify something that worked and why it worked) • I'm interested in learning (or hearing) more about... • I'd love to hear more about... • Thank you for sharing your thoughts. Can you tell me more about...?
Clarifying stems	**Probing stems**
• Let me see if I understand... • I'd be interested in hearing more about... • It would help me understand if you'd give me an example of... • So, are you saying/suggesting...? • Tell me what you mean when you... • Tell me how that idea is like (or different from)... • To what extent is...? • I'm curious to know more about... • I'm intrigued by... • I'm interested in... • I wonder...	• What's another way you might...? • What would it look like if...? • What do you think would happen if...? • How was...different from (or similar to)...? • What's another way you might...? • What sort of an impact do you think...? • What criteria do you use to...? • When have you done something like... before? • What do you think...? • How did you decide...(come to that conclusion?)? • I'm curious to know more about... • I'm intrigued by... • I'm interested in... • I wonder...

Table 2. General coaching sentence stems (adopted from Aguilar, 2013)

The coach intentionally fosters equality in the relationship, as opposed to pulling hierarchical rank. The coach seeks to work together with rather than directing the teacher. The coach offers choices, and seeks to build teacher voice and efficacy. Reflection on the part of the teacher becomes the critical component. The coach seeks to enable authentic dialogue based on the data derived from the student work and teacher's thinking.

In addition, with specific feedback the coach creates opportunities for teachers to practice and hone their skill in a new strategy. The coach invites the teacher to practice the skills immediately. Through coaching, video recording, and reflection the teacher receives immediate feedback and makes modifications if necessary (Knight, 2011).

Modeling active listening

We have discussed the importance of effective listening and paraphrasing in the first section of this book. Listening skills are paramount in the coach's work with teachers. In addition to the steps of paraphrasing which are discussed in Chapter 2, coaches should always:

1. commit themselves to listening;
2. make sure their partner is the speaker; and
3. think before they speak and ask themselves, "Will my comment open up or close down this conversation?" (Knight, 2011, p. 212).

In line with this disposition of mind, Costa & Garmston discuss the need for "a nonjudgmental, developmental, reflective model" designed to mediate "a practitioner's thinking, perceptions, beliefs and assumptions towards the goals of self-directed earning and increased complexity of cognitive processing" (2002, p. 5). Conversations involve planning, reflecting on teaching, or problem solving. Planning questions that are strategically linked to data and areas of professional practice is important if teacher's efficacy, collaboration, and professional satisfaction is to grow (Costa & Garmston, 2002, p. 23).

WHAT DATA TO COLLECT TO SUPPORT COACHING CONVERSATIONS

1. *Behavior*: Watch for how teachers set and teach expectations for quality of work and behavior to their students; how they build an environment of invitation and inclusion, and how they maximize positive student participation

2. *Content knowledge*: Look for indicators and evidence of standards driving the planning and the instruction; look for accuracy, depth, and higher-level thinking opportunities embedded within the content.

3. *Direct instruction*: Be conscious of the kind of activator a teacher uses to connect the students' prior background or current interest to the lesson at hand, the type of thinking which the teacher models for the students, the levels of thinking that the students are engaged in, the type of transformational activities which require students to interact with each other and content materials to make long-term meaning of the lesson.

4. *Formative assessment*: Capture the embedded, ongoing formative assessments which the teacher uses within the lesson as well as summative assessments at the end of the unit. Note how the collected evidence of student learning modifies the instruction.

GROWTH MODEL

Once you have collected evidence you looked for, your intention is to foster conversations with the teacher to support their growth in response to the data collected. Consider the Sir John Whitmore's growth model (Table 3) as a guide for your work with teachers.

> **Goal** setting for the session as well as short and long term
>
> What do you want to achieve?
> What do you want from this meeting?
> What do you want to learn more about?
>
> **Reality** checking to explore the current situation
>
> What is happening?
> Why is it a problem?
> What have you tried? What happened?
> How do you feel about that?
>
> **Options** and alternative strategies on courses of action
>
> What options do you think there are?
> What have you tried?
> What are the pros and cons?
> Is there anything else you can do?
>
> **What** is to be done, **when**, by **whom**, and the **will** to do it.

Table 3. GROWTH model questions (source: Whitmore, 2009, p. 55)

In addition to the GROWTH model, these questions can spur the teacher's thinking and anticipation skills:

Can you summarize what you are going to do and when?
What obstacles and objections might you anticipate?
How would you overcome them?
Who might provide support?
What resources do you think you will need?
When should we review the progress?

COACHING CONVERSATIONS

Robyn Jackson (2008) highlights four kinds of conversations between the coach and the teacher:

1. *Reflecting conversations*, in which the coach identifies teacher's behavior, beliefs, understanding, and how they affect events in their classroom. The coach paraphrases as a way of checking her or his understanding of the teacher's current thinking. The outcome is clarity.

2. *Facilitating conversations* serve to clarify goals. The coach uses clarifying questions to identify goals whose achievement will result in teacher's growth.

The outcome of this kind of conversation is goal setting.

3. *Coaching conversations* are designed to help a teacher realize why she or he is making progress or not. These conversations may suggest strategies or identify corrections or additions. The desired outcome is growth.

4. *Directing conversations* are designed to give a teacher clear instructions and tell her or him what the consequences are if they are not followed. The outcome is action.

Table 4 highlights the combinations of will (how motivated the teacher is to learn and change) and skill (does the teacher know how to learn and change, how to get better?) that can guide a coaching conversation. Ultimately, it is the role of the coach to inspire and motivate teachers to grow and increase their pedagogical capacity to improve student learning and achievement. This is the power of coaching.

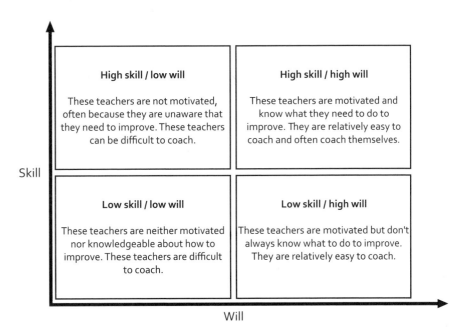

Table 4. Teacher's skill and will
(source: Marzano et al., 2013)

WHAT LEADERSHIP FOR INSTRUCTIONAL COACHING LOOKS LIKE

As an instructional leader you should:

1. model instructional focus and mindful presence as a precondition for effective coaching.

2. use the "Coaching Conversation Analysis Tool" designed by Aguilar (2013)[1] to observe and provide feedback to the teachers' coaches on teachers' skills of listening, questioning, and providing feedback.

3. practice the art of dialogue and inquiry by seeking to understand while withholding judgement in the conversation.

4. look for opportunities to foster connections between coaches, teachers, and faculty in general.

5. discuss the conditions for a meaningful conversation: humility, hope, faith, critical thinking, and love.

6. ask yourself how would our school be different if we prohibited verbal defamation and gossip? If we only spoke of the good you know of in other people and encourage others to do the same?

7. embrace and model six beliefs about coaching: I see others as equal partners in conversations; I believe people should have a lot of autonomy; I want to hear what others have to say; I don't judge my conversation partners; conversation should be back and forth; conversation should be life-giving (Knight, 2016).

8. strive to be authentic, consistent with what you believe as a leader and champion for students and their learning.

9. use the questions to ask a coach-applicant proposed by Aguilar (2013)[2] to make sure you hire a person with the right skillset to fill this important position.

10. develop a coaching vision and mission statement (see Aguilar's Mission/Vision Creation Tool[3]).

---

[1] available at: http://elenaaguilar.com/wp-content/uploads/2016/04/coaching_conversation_analysis_tool.pdf

[2] available at: http://elenaaguilar.com/wp-content/uploads/2016/04/Interview-Questions-for-Hiring-a-Coach.pdf

[3] available at: http://elenaaguilar.com/wp-content/uploads/2016/04/Coaching-Vision-Mission.docx

Chapter 10 / Coaching Conversations

STRATEGIES TO DEVELOP COACHING SKILL AND CONVERSATION

1. Watch the following video entitled "Observing and reflecting"[4].
2. Describe the main components of the coaching session between Ms. Tabor and Ms. Gonzalez. What are the benefits of each component?
3. How does Ms. Tabor benefit from her planning session with her coach?
4. Watch the video entitled, "Learning from Feedback"[5] and discuss how your team or department incorporates feedback into your current practice.
5. Consider video recording in your own classroom to expand your depth of reflection and instructional skill. Watch the video which models this process.[6]
6. Investigate the tips for video recording and analyzing your own teaching practice. Then record your own lesson and share your conclusions with your colleagues as a next step. Learn tips for recording video in your classroom.[7]
7. Consider the use of student feedback[8] as a valuable set of data to reflect upon, share with your coach, and use for planning for the future.
8. As a team or department, read the article entitled, Teacher Collaboration: The Essential Common-Core Ingredient By Vicki Phillips & Robert L. Hughes.[9]
9. Discuss how the work of a coach specifically links to student learning goals and school improvement goals. Make a direct connection between actions, expenditure of time, and support of those goals.
10. Use the Instructional Coach Self-Assessment Activity[10] to assess your strengths and areas of need as a coach in relation to the attributes of effective coaches.
11. Discuss how you adjust your approach to coaching to meet the needs of a particular situation, client, and the program's intended outcome.
12. Provide technical coaching about specific instructional practices using a checklist such as classroom observation checklist[11].

---

4 available at https://www.teachingchannel.org/videos/instructional-coaching-nvps
5 available at: https://www.teachingchannel.org/videos/benefits-coaching-teamwork-nvps
6 available at: https://www.teachingchannel.org/videos/use-video-to-improve-teaching-ousd
7 available at: https://www.teachingchannel.org/videos/videotaping-tips-for-teachers
8 for details visit: https://www.teachingchannel.org/videos/improve-teaching-with-student-feedback
9 available at: http://www.edweek.org/ew/articles/2012/12/05/13hughes.h32.html
10 available at: https://learningforward.org/docs/coachingmatters/killiontoolch3-4.pdf
11 available at: https://learningforward.org/docs/coachingmatters/killiontoolch4-4.pdf

BIBLIOGRAPHY

Aguilar, E. (2013). *The Art of Coaching: Effective Strategies for School Transformation*. San Francisco, CA: Jossey-Bass.

Biancarosa, G., Bryk, A. S., & Dexter, E. R. (2010). Assessing the Value-Added Effects of Literary Collaborative Professional Development on Student Learning. *The Elementary School Journal*, 111(1), 7–34.

Costa, A., & Garmston, R. (2002). *Cognitive Coaching: A Foundation for Renaissance Schools*. Norwood, MA: Christopher-Gordon.

Gawande, A. (2011). Personal best: Top Athletes and Singers Have Coaches. Should You? *The New Yorker*, 87(30), 44–53. Retrieved from: http://www.newyorker.com/magazine/2011/10/03/personal-best.

Jackson, R. (2008). *The Instructional Leader's Guide to Strategic Conversations With Teachers*. Washington, DC: Mindsteps Inc.

Joyce, B., & Showers, B. (2002). *Student Achievement Through Staff Development*. Alexandria, VA: Association for Supervision and Curriculum Development.

Killion, J., & Harrison, C. (2006). *Taking the Lead: New Roles for Teachers and Schoolbased Coaches*. Oxford, OH: National Staff Development Council.

Killion, J., Harrison, C., Bryan, C., & Clifton, H. (2012). *Coaching Matters*. Oxford, OH: Learning Forward.

Kise, J. (2006). *Differentiated Coaching: A Framework for Helping Teachers Change*. Thousand Oaks, CA: Corwin Press.

Knight, J. (2007). *Instructional Coaching: A Partnership Approach to Improving Instruction*. Thousand Oakes, CA: Corwin Press.

Knight, J. (2011). *Unmistakable Impact*. Thousand Oaks, CA: Corwin Press.

Knight, J. (2016). *Better Conversations: Coaching Ourselves and Each Other to be More Credible, Caring, and Connected*. Thousand Oaks, CA: Corwin Press.

Marzano, R. J., & Simms, J. A., Roy, T., Heflebower, T., & Warrick, P. (2013). *Coaching Classroom Instruction*. Bloomington, IN: Marzano Research Laboratory.

Nidus, G., & Sadder, M. (2011). The Principal as Formative Coach. *Educational Leadership*, 69(2), 30–35.

Phillips, V., & Hughes, R. L. (2012). Teacher Collaboration: The Essential Common-Core Ingredient. *Education Week*, 32(13), 32–33.

Vanderburg, M., & Stephens, D. (2010). The Impact of Literacy Coaches: What Teachers Value and How Teachers Change. *Elementary School Journal*, 111(1), 143–162.

Whitmore, J. (2009). *Coaching for Performance: GROWing Human Potential and Purpose – the Principles and Practice of Coaching and Leadership* (4th ed.). London: Nicholas Brealey Publishing.

Addressing Mediocre Teaching

> *I've come to a frightening conclusion that I am the decisive element in the classroom. It's my personal approach that creates the climate. It's my daily mood that makes the weather. As a teacher, I possess a tremendous power to make a child's life miserable or joyous. I can be a tool of torture or an instrument of inspiration. I can humiliate or heal. In all situations, it is my response that decides thether a crisis will be escalated or de-escalated and a child h umanized or dehumanized.*
>
> Haim G. Ginott (1975)

Instructional leaders are well aware of research showing that when students receive expert instruction, they can move from the 60th to the 96th percentile of learning, and when the instruction is ineffective, they can regress to the 3rd percentile by the end of their time with that teacher (Marzano, 2001, Saunders & Horn, 1998). This research highlights the power of teaching. It also highlights the importance of instructional leaders' number one role as student advocates—they ensure that there is an expert instructor in every classroom.

But what does an instructional leader do when the teacher isn't skillful but isn't downright hurting kids either? We call that mediocre teaching, which can be defined as instruction that is not good enough to help most children make progress and not bad enough to be grounds for contract termination. The question for every instructional leader to answer is how much mediocrity are you willing to accept in your school?

To address mediocrity one has to diagnose it first, to use the medical metaphor. Mediocrity is a condition with many variations. Each variation requires different supervisory response. This chapter is different from the rest in that it brings a series of six case studies of mediocre teaching. Each case requires a different supervisory response. Read these cases and think about what versions of these cases might currently exist in your school. In what ways have you addressed mediocrity? What results have your responses yielded? What may be the next steps to consider?

Case study 1: Paula Positive—a "people person"—endeared by students and colleagues but teaches at the surface level

Diagnosis: lack of teaching expertise

Overview

Paula Positive has been teaching the 3rd grade for nine years. The principal hired Paula because she was a "natural" when it came to building relationships with students. The principal determined that she would best provide the type of positive environment this grade level lacked. She would restore fun to learning and working together. Driven by the desire to bring this breath of fresh air to the grade level and the staff, the principal decided to overlook some of the less favorable aspects of Paula's background. Some of her interview responses and scores on her student-teaching evaluations indicated that she lacked expertise in some areas of practice, planning standards-based instruction in particular.

Paula was superficial in her understanding of the curriculum and needed to do more to address the needs of her higher performing students. This concern was also raised informally by some of the parents who felt their children were not being challenged enough or were learning things that they had already mastered. The principal's evaluation notes also reflected that Paula utilized instructional units and activities tied to themes and seasons without evidence of how the activities were tied to curriculum standards throughout the year. More and more parents were requesting at the beginning of the school year to have their child moved from Paula's classroom to other 3rd grade classrooms with teachers known to offer more rigor and substance in their teaching approach.

What is it like for the students?

There is a sense of community in Paula's classroom. The students seem to feel welcome, safe, and comfortable. Paula makes a concerted effort to create this environment. The students report that she is a "friendly" and "nice" teacher and they like coming to school because of her. Lower performing students benefit from her classes more because of the nurturing environment that she provides and the confidence they gain, but her instructional plans fail to meet the academic needs of other student sub-groups. In fact, Paula's written plans do not even recognize the need for different instruction and learning styles in her class. Paula writes learning objectives that describe the activities she conducts with no real connection to the curriculum targets for the third grade. Students in her class do not understand the larger purpose of their activities and can't internalize what they're really supposed to be able to do or what they should understand as a result of their learning experiences. Even though there very well may be many connections between her activity-based student learning experiences and the actual curriculum standards, she demonstrates an inconsistent understanding of how to plan instruction and that students need to be aware of, if not play a role in developing the learning goals and the larger roadmap as well.

Her students' backgrounds and prior performances or abilities do not seem to play a role in her planning at all. Every year she spends the first six weeks of the school year on units that review things the students should have already learned in the second grade, regardless of whether the review is necessary or not. After the review phase, she moves on to a series of "holiday celebration" thematic units that run from Columbus Day through Easter/Spring. Again, the units and teaching materials are not connected to the curriculum, the students are not aware of what they're really learning, and she makes no attempt to extend or modify the learning experiences based on students' needs or any kind of informal or formal student data whatsoever. Despite all of this, if you were to walk into Paul's classroom at any given moment, you would observe students experiencing a classroom full of fun-filled, interactive, and even hands-on learning. Students would be engaged, smiling, encouraged, cooperating, and on-task. Even if they tell you that the work is "too easy", without a more in-depth conversation with them you would never know from the "looks of things" that the instruction is so lacking.

Considerations for supervision

Paula's example comes into view during a time in education where the stakes are high. Teaching technique and instructional design are highly scrutinized, as they should be. You could say that she never should have been given tenure or that if the original principal had brought her shortcomings to light from the beginning, this situation never would have continued, and now she is set in her ways and it is too late to change her. Paula is a classic example of a teacher who was granted permanent status because she filled a perceived need, because the teaching pool lacked and there was a larger risk involved with replacing Paula, and/or because the supervisor made a poor decision. Paula presents a challenge because her effort is immense but not effective, because she seems to whole-heartedly believe she is doing what is right for the students, and because a pattern has been established where Paula has not received the feedback she needs and was never given the opportunity to reflect.

For the first decade of her career, the leadership she has worked with was strongly focused on her strengths and ignored the skills she lacked, and therefore, a decade of students did not receive the instruction they needed. In the current culture of education, this is malpractice and can no longer be ignored. Paula has more than half of her teaching career still ahead of her. The challenge is to help her see the connection between her strengths and weaknesses. Paula needs to understand that she can still be an advocate of her students' feelings and emotional well-being, that a love of learning can still be cultivated, and that she will still be successful at maintaining the on-task behavior of her class when she steps out of her own comfort zone and learns how to become a teacher who holds children accountable for their learning and who provides well-designed standards-based instruction and carefully constructed learning experiences.

Effective leader responses

Build on Paula's strengths (much of what she does naturally in the area of classroom management can't be taught). Help her to recognize classroom management as one of the key elements to promoting student learning.

Raise expectations (everyone has the potential to learn and grow throughout their career). Be specific and direct about where Paula can improve to make professional growth more attainable.

Give clear feedback that is based on her techniques as an educator rather than her personality. Provide examples of the improvements that are needed (e.g., provide specific data from observation about the types of questions being asked and give specific examples for the types of questions with low or no usage).

Establish clear goals and benchmarks for assessing progress in the identified areas and delineate who will do what. Schedule the next evaluation conversation and set reasonable goals until then.

Surround Paula with reflective educators and a collaborative culture in her grade level.

Invest time and resources and balance them with realistic expectations.

Focus on curriculum planning and instructional design as a larger school initiative.

Even small steps are progress, as they can have a significant effect and will encourage future development. Failure to improve is not an option.

Case study 2: Donna Dogandpony—an unprepared educator who is "flying on fumes" and making it up as she goes along

Diagnosis: lack of teaching depth

Overview

Donna Dogandpony has been teaching middle school science for 22 years. She is mostly thought of by her supervisors as an engaging teacher who makes learning fun. At first glance she seems competent. She has positive relationships with her past and present students.

Donna is an organized person, who runs an orderly and efficient classroom. Classroom management is definitely her strength. She understands the importance of classroom procedures and knows how to create and implement them. Her classroom runs like a well-oiled machine. Her lessons are organized too—on the surface. She has taught the same units for 22 years and she knows how to put her plans on paper. However, her lessons lack depth both in her written plans and her delivery. Her written plans are mostly composed of notes referencing textbooks or other instructional materials. For the learning objectives of a particular lesson she often references a page number of the text book, for example the plans will say, "Objectives: See page 27." Lessons lack details about the content-specific, step-bystep procedures for the strategies. There is a lack of planning for specific questions and discussion stems. No evidence of planning for specific student learning needs is present either. She finds curriculum standards to match her "hobby teaching" of the same beloved teaching units that she uses year in and year out. It is apparent when reviewing her lesson plans that little to no forethought is given to her lessons. It can also be concluded that she does not know how to use curriculum standards or establish learning objectives. The lessons that she teaches often play out completely different from what she has written in her plan book. Her actual teaching is planned on the fly and/or made up as she goes along. She has commented on several occasions that she feels her best teaching comes from "teachable moments" or "reading her students" and "changing it up"—whatever "it" is supposed to be.

The consequences of Donna's lack of planning can be seen in the classroom in a myriad of ways. One of the most affected areas is the way she questions students during all phases of her lessons. Questions are incoherent and their purpose unclear. Most of the random questions asked are basic recall questions. Student responses are largely overlooked anyway—she is asking to ask, not asking to truly listen. Sometimes the students do not understand her questions and require clarification before they can answer, even at the recall level.

Donna's limited and arbitrary approach to planning is directly linked to another problem area—inadequate background knowledge of her content. The type of teaching license she was initially granted is no longer available. She holds a K-8 License for General Education. At the time when she began teaching, this qualified her to teach middle school science, and she is now grandfathered in it. Prior to graduating with her teacher degree, Donna completed course work for general methods in teaching science and other areas but received no specific training to teach middle school science. Her lack of content knowledge is no doubt the root of her issues with planning and execution of planned lessons (i.e., lack of appropriate questioning, failure to facilitate class discussions, and inability to engage students for a sustained period of time.

What is it like for the students and parents?

When students or parents question Donna, she perceives the parent or student as overbearing, showing off, or trying to divert attention from the student's underperformance in her class. There is often excitement on days when one of her infamous "hobby teaching" projects is going to take place. Opportunities for students to work one-on-one with Donna are rare. Some students respond well and react positively to the high volume of small group projects. Some feel that there is way too much "team time" and are bored with it, and others feel like they are always pulling more of the weight than their peers. There is no variation in her lesson plans to address specific student learning needs prior to, during, or after teaching a lesson (such as using an additional visual aid or trying a different way to explain a problem). Donna doesn't align teaching materials, curriculum standards, and student needs, which creates a very monotonous learning experience for students.

Student anxiety levels are high, and they are very apprehensive when given assessments that require writing. They have trouble composing essays in response to written prompts. Her students are used to being assessed as a group due to all of the team projects and group work that she utilizes. Students are also used to answering basic questions through poorly developed and or textbook-provided multiple-choice questions. Donna always uses multiple-choice, true-false, traditional textbook assessments and never ventures into the "alternative assessments" section of the materials, let alone create her own. Students do well when they're asked to memorize facts. They can even create index cards they can use on the test but don't do well when the questions require any application whatsoever of the concepts learned. Some students have also vocalized a perception that Donna favors students who don't ask a lot of questions. In fact, some students in her classes have even been known to pretend they understand less than they actually do.

Donna is resentful about being asked to attend what she believes to be "endless" professional development about the ever-changing curriculum. She deems it to be some arbitrary fad. She believes that the latest iteration of standards was created to scapegoat educators by forcing them to teach for the test. She masks her own incompetency in the area of assessment with the claim that we are over-testing our students and that "enough is enough." If there is "too much" of it, then she thinks she really doesn't need to know anything about it at all. She does not see a role for it in her instructional process.

Considerations for supervision

Donna presents a common supervisory challenge, which is that she has gotten by for so long without anybody drawing her attention to any of the areas of her mediocre teaching. In other words, she has received neutral or positive feedback, but no specific areas needing improvement have been brought to her attention. The challenge to effectively supervise Donna is twofold. The first is to get Donna to see her own need for growth after years of complacent belief that she was a very successful educator. The second is to get past her argument that these "necessary improvements" have never been mentioned to her before and therefore she has had no need to change anything that she has been doing. As far as she was told, her planning and instructional design skills and level of content knowledge were fine and actually referred to her as strengths. She hasn't changed anything she is doing, so why are her reviews changing? This perception supports her feeling that it's not her performance that is the issue, but the goal posts that have changed. And her feeling is, they will be changed back again as well.

Effective leader responses

Ask teaching teams to regularly share and/or co-plan instructional units tied to curriculum standards and to integrate a variety of curriculum resources. In addition, have teams check the alignment between standards and existing curriculum materials and programs such as textbooks in order to identify gaps. Provide opportunities for professional growth, support, and resources that show educators how to do this, especially when new sets of standards are released.

Plan with longer templates and periodically request and review the templates. Work in teams and with committees to create your school's own customized long-form planning templates that address your school's specific instructional design needs and goals and curriculum standards.

Routinely collect and analyze assessments to evaluate what types are being used and match them to the learning goals that need to be measured. Look for places where different types of assessments are needed, because the results don't really tell you what you need to know. Adapt pre-written assessments and create new assessments with teams of teachers.

Collect and evaluate random sample of student work from Donna's class.

Require evidence of ongoing professional growth as well as evidence of reflection about what was learned and how it will be applied. Require goals based on professional development and periodically review those goals. Help teachers identify where resources to achieve those goals are inadequate and use that information to identify future professional development opportunities.

Surround Donna with reflective educators and a collaborative culture in her grade level.

Invest time and resources and balance them with realistic expectations.

Focus on curriculum planning and instructional design as a larger school initiative.

Even small steps are progress, as they can have a significant effect and will encourage future development. Failure to improve is not an option.

Case study 3: Leon Linebacker—coaching is the "real job"—cares only about sports and believes that teaching (anything but social studies) is just a means to an end (and a way to play out his football fantasies)

Diagnosis: misguided beliefs about the purpose of education

Overview

52 year-old Leon Linebacker has taught computer science for 23 years at a high school. During his tenure, Leon applied twice for the assistant principal position and two times for both the assistant and head athletic director positions. On all occasions the interview panel declined the application due to a lack of evidence that he possesses the necessary skills to work with and lead a team. He has been a well-liked and very respected head coach of a football team for the last 15 years. He is known as a coach who pushes his athletes on the field and doesn't shy away from competition. He values a winning attitude in his players and promotes (even favors) students who win. Despite the fact that a fair amount of students (and their parents) at the school feel discouraged and unwelcome in the school's athletic program because they are not "natural winners," his popularity and community support, based largely on his winning record and longevity at the helm, are unwavering.

Mr. Linebacker is methodical in his organization both in his classroom and on the field. Although he is most "alive" on the field, in his classroom he seems to be going through the motions. His grade book is both meticulous and monolithic, with quiz and test scores entered in a pattern. His weekly lesson plans are always completed in a timely and organized manner but are limited in their depth and mostly appear as brief notes about which topics will be covered. Mr. Linebacker appears to be bored with teaching. He seems disinterested in either student learning or his subject matter or perhaps both.

What is it like for the students?

Beside the fact that Mr. Linebacker's class is predictable, there is little else for students in his class to look forward to. They enter the classroom as an organized but very sterile setting. There are few decorations on the walls: a rules chart and some outdated posters touting cliché remarks (intended, yet failing to inspire), such as "Winners Never Quit." Consistently, what the students experience day in day out (other than on quiz and test days) is rapid-fire drills and recall questions based on the previous day's homework and reading assignments. Athletes and male students are given preferential and lenient treatment for late assignments and incomplete work, whereas non-athletes are held to a higher standard regarding their assignments and held more accountable for underperforming during the daily "learning drills". Mr. Linebacker will sometimes even make comments to suggest that the athletes work hard for the school on the field, and that the "academic types" need to carry their share of weight "off the field". All of the students call Mr. Linebacker "coach" in class. It is blatantly obvious to the students what the "coach's" priority is, and it's not computer science.

Considerations for supervision

As an educator nearing retirement, Leon represents an ongoing challenge for supervisors. Most educators like him were athletes themselves as high school and college students. They went to college to play sports and wanted to continue a life in sports. Since you can't major in coaching, the easiest way to be a coach of a high school sports team is to become a teacher. They didn't choose to major in secondary education for the love of a subject. The desired career path for Leon and other individuals like him was to eventually become the "coach" or manager of the whole school or athletic director, as all that it takes is being a good coach, that is, a "leader". As a tenured, veteran teacher his career may seem to be winding down, but since coaching is his life, he won't be going anywhere anytime soon.

Effective leader responses

Accept that Leon isn't going anywhere, that there are not enough grounds for disciplinary action, and that the situation in the classroom is never going to improve on its own or from subtle approaches. Direct and purposeful action is required.

Engage Leon in a meeting about helping him achieve his future goals, separate and apart from the evaluation process and conferences.

Help Mr. Linebacker refocus some of his energy for coaching back onto the classroom by pointing out to him as a seasoned teacher and coach that successful coaching and how a coach motivates his players is the same reflective process as the one a teacher should apply. Help him connect the self-improvement process he goes through as a coach to something that can work for him as a teacher as well. Enlist his help in sharing this method with his colleagues.

Invite Leon to take on leadership roles on school committees. Make sure strong role models are on the committees too. Explain what the duties of leading the committee are and explain to Mr. Linebacker how his experience will help him succeed in his ultimate career goal as administrator as well.

When you encounter Leon, shift the conversation away from the ordinary topic of coaching. Have brief "hallway meetings" and make sure the conversations are focused on teaching.

Case study 4: Louise Lowbar—lowers expectations for select groups of students

Diagnosis: discriminating low expectations

Overview

Louise Lowbar has taught the 7th and 8th grade English at a middle school for 18 years. She is organized, enthusiastic, and one of the most popular teachers at the school. Mrs. Lowbar is well respected in the community as well. This school is a Title I school with students coming from a variety of socio-economic backgrounds. Mrs. Lowbar and her husband live in one of the more affluent resort-style subdivisions located within the school's zone. It is a golf course community and her husband is a real-estate developer. His company helped build the community clubhouse and he sits on the club's board of directors. The two are very active and involved in the community charitable and political circles. Due to her public persona, Mrs. Lowbar is very well liked.

She thinks of herself as a person who deeply cares about what she calls "at-risk" students. Especially the students whose families are facing economic challenges. In fact, a great deal of her charitable work in the community is for an organization that collects toy donations and coats during the winter holidays, provides meals in the summer time to fill the gap when students aren't receiving school meals, and collects used books in good condition and redistributes them to families in need. Mrs. Lowbar sits on the organization's board and spends her free time volunteering for the organization. She feels like she has a great deal of empathy for these students, which is why she always pays attention to any special needs they might have. She groups her students based on their backgrounds and other factors that might put them at a disadvantage and she can be heard in the staff lounge saying things like "those are my low-ability kids—the ones that mostly live in the Woods or Shady Side." The Woods is a mobile home subdivision and Shady Side is a lower-income housing development both within the schools' attendance zone. Louise often talks about what she changes in the classroom because of her perceived needs of these students. She gives them the first five minutes of class for "prep time". In her class this is the time to "ready" yourself for learning. Students are allowed to use this free time to go to the bathroom, sharpen pencils, locate supplies, talk to neighbors, sit quietly, or finish up homework they couldn't do the night before. Mrs. Lowbar says that students need to be able to decompress after their stressful home lives so it's worth the missed instructional time.

She hesitates to give honest feedback to students or ask them to correct or improve their writing because she doesn't want to hurt their feelings and she reduces the requirements for nightly reading because the students' home lives are way to chaotic to be able to concentrate on reading. Which is another reason why her students get the first five minutes of class for the "prep time". She also says that report cards aren't fair when certain students just don't have the ability to do certain work or achieve certain standards. She often inflates report card grades and avoids calling home. She feels that her "low-ability" students already have enough trouble in their lives, as they come from broken families with little or no family support. She doesn't want to embarrass them or make the situation worse by giving low grades or calling on them during class discussions. Her other students who are not labeled as "low-ability" are required to work with greater depth, rigor, and intellectual stimulation. Louise is oblivious to the fact that these low expectations actually harm her students and undermine her efforts to help this population with her charitable work.

What is it like for the students?

The students are aware of the differences in the way Mrs. Lowbar treats them. Mrs. Lowbar doesn't make comments in front of the whole class, but there is some evidence that she may mention things to the students who are not in the "low-ability" group. None of her students mention it or complain of the unfairness, but by the way they act in the class, you can tell that they realize there are differences in what they are expected to do. There are students who are always called on and students who don't even raise their hands. Class jobs and extra responsibilities aren't given to the low-ability group, because Mrs. Lowbar doesn't want to put anything "extra" on their plates. On one occasion, a student who was distributing homework assignments in the class mail folders was asked by an attending adult why some classmates got less homework. The student responded by whispering, "The low kids don't get as much homework."

The students in Mrs. Lowbar's class exhibit a great deal of respect and caring for her and for each other. The class feels connected to one another. It is not likely that the whole class would exclude or ridicule the group of "low-ability" students, but it is also clear that the conversations Mrs. Lowbar has with the parents in her social circles are being overheard and repeated by some of her students. It is also possible that her very perceptive 7th and 8th graders are just noticing that Mrs. Lowbar has lowered expectations for some of their peers.

Considerations for supervision

Addressing this type of mediocre teaching is challenging. It is difficult to recognize, and if recognized, it is equally difficult to define and explain. The problem is even more challenging if the expectations are lowered for an entire group of students. When this practice is embedded in the culture of the school, it is a feat to change. Strong leadership is required. The leader must first be aware and able to document the instances in order to demonstrate a pattern. The leader must also be willing to share her or his findings with Mrs. Lowbar, even if it might be embarrassing. He or she must also be prepared to shift the culture at the school so that Louise and other educators are able to reflect, discuss, and ultimately change the way they are setting and communicating expectations.

Since Louise doesn't find anything wrong with her own behavior, follow-up will be needed. She is agreeable when suggestions are given, such as at the end of the school year after testing scores are discussed. However, most often, she never uses the suggestions and ends up falling back on the same excuses about why they don't work. Due to her connections in the community, the parents don't complain. Even the parents who may be inclined to voice concerns, because their children are treated differently, rarely do. All of her students are getting average or better grades, are behaving in class, and all really like their teacher. Louise is an ineffective or mediocre teacher because of an underlying, subconscious system of beliefs. Her students are being shortchanged despite her best intentions. The matter is serious and the principal will need to be prepared to make direct and documented recommendations or directives. The principal must also be prepared to address this problem on a schoolwide level in a way that raises the tide and lifts Louise with it.

Effective leader responses

Recognize that Louise is part of a larger institutional problem. Address Louise's issue both individually and as a part of a school-wide shift and focus. Many educators are often unaware that they are lowering their expectations. Help the entire faculty eliminate hidden bias when setting expectations.

Increase family and community engagement as part of the school-wide focus. Ask parents and caregivers what they believe best helps children to learn and succeed.

Provide school-wide professional development courses to study and understand the bias that exists and figure out how to eliminate the bias.

Use a variety of data to formally evaluate Louise and the rest of the staff. Base the conversations about expectations and biases on facts and evidence.

Establish clear goals and benchmarks for assessing progress in the identified areas.

Case study 5: Harry Hatespeople—whines and complains constantly and believes collaboration is a waste of time

Diagnosis: sabotaging a collaborative environment among the adults

Overview

Harry Hatespeople is known to be a strong high school mathematics teacher. With a doctoral degree in mathematics, he is very knowledgeable of his subject area and well prepared for each lesson he teaches. He has a great relationship with his students and is respected by the parents as well. Harry has a firm grasp of the various ways that students learn. When someone isn't "getting something" in one of his classes, he knows what to do. He has high expectations of his students and believes all students are capable of meeting those expectations. His lessons are rigorous, and he is fair. He uses ongoing formative assessment to inform his instructional decisions. He meets with students every other day during his lunch period to provide extra help and answer questions. He is well versed in the state standards for mathematics. Harry is succinct and methodical as he pulls together all of the necessary components of instructional design that an educator goes through.

Mr. Hatespeople's formal observations and evaluations have been positive and he has exhibited growth as an educator in the role of "teaching". It is the other roles of an educator where we can start to see issues. He believes that all of the things that teachers are expected to do outside of the classroom are a waste of time and a distraction from the important work. He does not like to collaborate with his colleagues. He is completely unwilling to share the vast amount of teaching strategies and deep content knowledge he possesses with others. He strongly prefers to work in isolation when he's not in his classroom. Mr. Hatespeople interacting with his students and Mr. Hatespeople interacting with his colleagues could not be two more different persons.

What is it like for the students?

The reputation of Mr. Hatespeople's class is that you have to make an effort and work hard, and if you do that, you will succeed in his class. He is seen as serious but approachable. Students like his straightforward approach, his clarity, and his willingness to work with them when they are confused. Students feel that if they put in the extra work, then Mr. Hatespeople will too. Students would say that if he explains things one way and you don't understand, he quickly responds with another way of looking at it. He can keep going until he finds your light switch. One year, he complained when he was assigned one 9th grade math class to teach. He said the students were too immature. From that point forward the department chair asked the principal to assign the extra 9th grade math class to someone else.

Considerations for supervision

School leaders have to be able to make the case for how collaborating with colleagues translates to school improvement. If the behavior of a teacher like Mr. Hatespeople goes unchecked, it could bring down the culture of the entire school. Collecting data about this issue could prove challenging, as there is rarely any evidence. The conversations that Harry has take place outside of the supervisor's earshot (e.g., parking lot, staff lounge, or lunchroom). Regardless of where the negativity occurs, the weight of it is pulling down the strong community of professionals at the school. Unfortunately, only Mr. Hatespeople's students will benefit from his knowledge and expertise.

When an educator is struggling in his or her own classroom, in most cases it is not public, and this privacy can sometimes make the problem easier to solve. However, when a person like Harry is struggling, it happens outside of the classroom and everyone knows what is going on. Some staff members are watching to see if this negativity will be tolerated. They are waiting for school leaders to act. Some staff members are ignoring it completely because they don't' want to get involved. Some may try to pick up the slack of the things he won't do. Eventually all three of these scenarios will build up resentment. Even if Harry is the only negative person or if there are a few more leaning his way, the potential to permeate a healthy school culture is real. Finally, it is important to remember that Harry is a young teacher, still in the first third of his career. It is really a make-or-break opportunity that this school has to shape Harry's belief system for the future.

Effective leader responses

Work to have your whole staff internalize standards for professional practice for educators. Either develop your own standards as a staff, use your school district's standards, or work with a national body of standards for the teaching profession. Conduct staff work around the various roles and responsibilities that educators fulfill both in and out of the classroom. Talk about these roles and identify why they are important for the students and the staff.

Develop and share a mission statement with the staff (as well as with staff members who work outside of the classroom, members of the school community, and students). Make sure the roles, responsibilities, and standards for professional practice are reflected in this statement (e.g. being a community of learners or supporting one another as professionals).

Have the staff or the supervisor assist you with developing a way to collect evidence that staff members are meeting the agreed standards of professional practice, which include non-classroom areas of performance. This will encourage educators to reflect about their performance outside of the classroom.

Invite Harry to help roll out new curriculum materials, make choices about curriculum materials, and/or work with new teachers to help them in curriculum design.

Ask for input from Harry about his concerns and focus on what he is complaining about and not on the way in which he is complaining. This should be your starting point for determining if a problem really exists and for finding solutions.

Meet with other colleagues in administration who also have to deal with resistance by faculty members and share strategies that work. Seek out individual strategies and strategies that can repair damage to the school culture and address the problem systemically.

Recognize Harry's effectiveness in the classroom, but at the same tell him loud and clear that you expect him to collaborate with other staff members as part of his professional responsibilities. Ask Harry what support he needs to make this happen.

Have Harry set goals around this issue. Follow up with self-evaluation benchmarks and conferences to discuss progress.

Case study 6: Sarah Stories—a "people person" endeared by students and colleagues but is chronically unprepared and wasting student instructional time due to personal problems

Diagnosis: letting private life interfere with work

Overview

Sarah Stories is a 5th grade teacher with eight years of teaching experience. The first six years of teaching were very successful for Sarah. She hit the ground running, and her students were well taught, and the school community was very positively influenced by her enthusiasm and dedication. She worked on the weekends to earn her master's degree during her second and third years of teaching. She was active on school committees. She volunteered to take on practicum students and became involved in mentoring new teachers. After her first year of teaching, she volunteered to co-chair the 5th grade level.

In the fifth year of her career, she hit a wall and she has been declining since that point. It began when she went through an unexpected and very hostile divorce. At first, it affected her professionalism. She began showing up late for work and not turning in her weekly lesson plans. Then she withdrew from meetings and became disorganized in her school leadership responsibilities. After the toll on her professionalism, negativity trickled into her classroom. At first, her principal believed that she would break through the wall and get back on track. However, the problems in Sarah's personal life continued. The divorce left her as a single mother of two. Her elder child, a high school student, began to have problems with her self-esteem and behaved recklessly. In addition, Sarah's mom was diagnosed with multiple sclerosis and instead of receiving help through a rough time, Sarah found herself struggling to find a way to help her mom even though she was barely holding things together herself. This vicious cycle continued, and Sarah sought council and support of her colleagues. The staff lounge became more like a group therapy session. Sarah got by for about a year because of her reputation with the families and admiration from the staff. By year seven, the principal realized how severe the problem was and how deeply it affected the students.

Considerations for supervision

One of the biggest challenges for this type of mediocrity is being able to distinguish between temporary bumps on the road and a pattern of steady decline. In the case of a temporary setback, you may have a teacher that acknowledges that she is going through something that may take all of her time and energy for a while. She may even ask the principal if someone could fill in as a grade-level chairperson for a month or so while she handles the personal setback. In the second case, the person gets so caught up in the decline that she doesn't even realize it's happening. She doesn't ask for help, and it becomes an ongoing situation that deteriorates over time. In both instances, principals must understand that they need to show empathy and support for their staff but at the same time quickly recognize if the setback is not temporary and has taken over that person's professional (and personal) life. Principals must also recognize that reversing the pattern of negativity is going to require direct intervention before it reaches Sarah's level. This instance is a true test of the leaders' convictions, because choosing to intervene on behalf of the students could be perceived as cold and uncaring about the staff. The principal must proceed in a way that is respectful of Sarah but is direct enough to change the circumstances. Furthermore, the principal must be supportive of Sarah while at the same time documenting and collecting evidence to demonstrate if she is meeting her goals for improvement or not.

Effective leader responses

Approach the situation with caution. Given the "public" nature of Sarah's situation, the staff is very concerned. The administrator's reaction could divide staff and draw a wedge between teachers and the leadership. Taking any action that seems cold and unsympathetic could cause anger and resentment while inaction and turning a blind eye could lead to cynicism and discontent. An effective leader will consider next steps carefully.

Show Sarah sympathy while still articulating the need to focus on the needs of the students.

Be direct, acknowledge Sarah's personal challenges, but do not accept them as an excuse for not doing her job the way that she is capable of (e.g., "I know that you have been going through some remarkably tough things over the last two years and it makes me feel sad to see this happening to you. I also see that you continue to overcome these challenges as they arrive. I want to see you teach like you used to before this all started two years ago. How can I help you do that?" Build on Sarah's strengths.

Develop a written plan that:

details a reasonable timeline for improvements;

- identifies performance areas that have been neglected;
- sets goals based on clear expectations;
- identifies benchmarks and documents progress toward these goals, including self-evaluation and conferences to discuss progress;
- acknowledges that it is time to move forward in the professional environment and away from all of the things that have happened in the past two years.
- includes methods, plans, or strategies for things the teacher can do outside of the school in order to help her separate personal problems for her work in the future (e.g., counseling, support group, etc.)

CONCLUSION

Once you decide to address mediocre teaching as an instructional leader, you may find yourself overwhelmed by how many forms it may take. You may have experienced teachers who abuse drugs and alcohol on the job, teachers who are physically declining so that they are not able to see, hear or respond appropriately to students, teachers who dislike students intensely and let the students know it, teachers who sabotage their colleagues to feed their own egos or those who give their time and attention to stirring up trouble with the teacher's union instead of providing high quality lessons to students. Whatever the situation, it is up to you to advocate for expert instruction in every classroom. Your passion for advocacy is critical. Your support for high-quality instruction, building collaborative structures which highlight great teaching, and fostering reflective conversation based on classroom data is critical. We end this chapter as we began, "How much mediocrity are you willing to accept on your watch as an instructional leader?"

BIBLIOGRAPHY

Ginott, H. G. (1975). *Teacher and Child: A Book for Parents and Teachers*. New York, NY: Macmillan.

Marzano, R. J. (2001.). *A New Era of School Reform: Going Where the Research Takes Us*. Aurora, CO: Mid-Continent Research for Education and Learning.

Platt, A., Tripp, C., Ogden, W. & Fraser, R. (2000). *The Skillful Leader: Confronting Mediocre Teaching*. Acton, MA: Ready about Press

Saunders, W. L., & Horn, S. P. (1998). Research Findings from the Tennessee Value-Added Assessment System (TVAAS) Database: Implications for Educational Evaluation and Research. *Journal of Personnel Evaluation in Education*, 12(3), 247–256.

SECTION 3

STRATEGIES FOR CONFIDENCE IN COMPLEX SITUATIONS

Navigating Through Change

ASSUMPTIONS ABOUT CHANGE
THE CHAOS OF CHANGE
RESISTANCE TO CHANGE
ORGANIZATIONAL CHALLENGES OF EMBRACING CHANGE
CHANGE AS A GRIEVING PROCESS
THE IMPLEMENTATION DIP
PLANNING FOR RESISTANCE

> *"It's not so much that we're afraid of change or so in love with the old ways, but it's that place in between that we fear... It's like being between trapezes... It's Linus when his blanket is in the dryer. There's nothing to hold on to."*
>
> Marilyn Ferguson

Change means that we replace something with something else, pass from one state or stage to another or one layer of knowing to another. Change means that we have to try something new, implement new skills, embrace a new way of doing things. In the process we abandon one routine or pattern for the sake of another, and leaving our zone of comfort often feels very uncomfortable. This is how Michael Fullan describes organizations coping with change:

> *For a long time, we have been finding that when organizations try something new, even if there has been some pre-implementation preparation, the first few months are bumpy. How could it be otherwise? New skills and understanding have a learning curve. Once we brought this out in the open, a lot of people immediately felt better knowing that it is normal and everyone goes through it. This finding led to the realization that we needed to focus on capacity building in this critical stage.*
> (2011, p. 71)

ASSUMPTIONS ABOUT CHANGE

A skillful instructional leader can plan change based on four assumptions. The first is that conflict and disagreement are not only inevitable but fundamental to successful change. This means that as a leader, you need to have a stomach not only to live through conflicts, disagreements, and potential standoffs but also to facilitate them.

The second assumption is that people need pressure to change, even in directions they desire. There are very few people who wake up and say, "Eureka! I need to change my life" and actually follow through with all that this decision implies. Leadership pressure to foster change is necessary even when change has a morally justified purpose and many good reasons on which everybody agrees. The initiative for change will only be effective if you allow people to react, form their own position, and interact with each other.

The third assumption is that effective change takes time. Two to three years for specific innovations, five or more for institutional reforms. This time variable depends on how ripe the faculty is to change, on their experience with earlier changes and risk taking, on their capacity and trust in it, on their current level of collaboration and the spirit of camaraderie and willingness to help each other out. The less you have of these, the more time it will take to change and the other way around.

The fourth assumption of any wise instructional leader is that if a change has been stalled, the real reason is not an outright rejection or hard-core resistance to all change. Instead, the more likely reasons are grief, fear, or lack of resources. A skilled instructional leader knows that supporting people through change means looking below the surface (remember the iceberg metaphor?).

THE CHAOS OF CHANGE

With true change inevitably comes chaos. At least at first. Some find this stage thrilling and like it the best. Others find it scary. If your working style as instructional leader is concrete, linear, and sequential, this may be a challenge. If yours is a learning style, more abstract and random, chaos may not be as difficult. Regardless, you and the faculty need to embrace chaos as a necessary element of change. Burke highlights the non-linear nature of change when he says that the implementation process is messy: "Things don't proceed exactly as planned; people do things their own way, not always according to plan; some people resist or even sabotage the process; and some people who would have been predicted to support or resist the plan actually behave in the opposite way. In short, unanticipated consequences occur" (2002, p. 2).

RESISTANCE TO CHANGE

This reality of human resistance to change is highlighted in an anecdotal exchange retold by Roland Barth (2002, p. XXIV):

TRANSMISSION

Please divert your course fifteen degrees north to avoid a collision.

RESPONSE

Recommend that YOU divert your course fifteen degrees south to avoid a collision.

TRANSMISSION

This is the captain of a U.S. Naval ship. I say again, divert your course.

RESPONSE

No, I say again, divert YOUR course.

TRANSMISSION

This is the aircraft carrier Enterprise. We are a large warship of the US Navy. Divert your course NOW!

RESPONSE

This is a lighthouse. Your call.

No matter what the stakes, it is the human nature to struggle with change, even if you asked for it. What if you were told that without change you would die? Ninety percent of the people who got the "change or die" warning did not change. Physicians, psychologists, and neuroscientists found that after their patients had heart bypass surgery, 90% did not change their diet, continued to avoid exercise, and didn't follow through with regular checkups. Seventy percent of these 90% had another heart attack and died (Deutschman, 2005). They simply couldn't bring themselves to change their lifestyle.

I work with many teachers and directors in independent schools around the world, where the culture is to move from one country or continent to another every three years on average. Even though they've sought out the new position and new country, regardless of how skilled and talented they are, change is daunting. Even the simplest procedure ("How do I request a substitute teacher when I am sick?") can feel overwhelming and humbling. Oftentimes I hear them say, "Whatever possessed me to think this was a good idea?" Change is hard. It challenges our capacity, our sense of self and our ego until we get to the other side of it.

ORGANIZATIONAL CHALLENGES OF EMBRACING CHANGE

In schools and school systems with extreme teacher autonomy, isolationist culture, and no common goals, change is next to impossible. There is no collective sense of what they are trying to accomplish, so change from one state or initiative to another is irrelevant. Equally, in highly congenial schools, characterized by people being happy, friendly, and kind to each other, there is still no infrastructure which invites and supports change. Just because people have legendary holiday parties doesn't mean that they have a common professional direction or purpose.

The only school infrastructure which supports real change from beginning to end, despite the anticipated human struggle through the process, is a highly collegial one (Ogden & Germinaro, 1995). In a highly collegial school, teachers have been used to and model a collaboration structure where they have been studying the data of teaching and learning today (DuFour, 2004; Love, 2008) and can identify areas that would be enhanced through change (Smith, 2008). They plan and discuss instructional strategies together and can identify where they need to alter course and modify their instruction for the betterment of students. Collegial schools are few and far between.

Even when a school is collegial, change is very personal and individualized. An instructional leader knows how to differentiate support to help people navigate through what ultimately is a personal journey (Garmston & Wellman, 2013). After all, to quote Hall and Hord, "...successful change starts and ends at the individual level. An entire organization does not change until each member has changed. Another way to say this is that there is an individual aspect to organizational change." (2006, p. 7)

CHANGE AS A GRIEVING PROCESS

A kindergarten teacher with forty years of experience waited for me after a day of training to ask if I could help her stage a case against the work of researcher and psychologist Lev Vygotsky and his famous zone of proximal development (1978). She wanted to share it with her principal to prove that the principal's idea for a new program based on Vygotsky's theories was a very bad idea. When I dug into what was really behind the request, I saw that she was asked to be trained in a different approach to working with her students than she had been used to for the past 40 years. Vygotsky happened to be quoted in the literature. Her fear, self-doubt, and worry as to if she had the capacity to evolve seemed too big to address. It seemed easier to take on Vygotsky. After I reminded her what a curious mind she has, that everyone in the team will be together learning these new skills, that no one will be comparing or competing, and that 80% of the game was just showing up, she calmed down. She was reminded of her capacity to learn and that she could meet this challenge.

That conversation reminded me of Elizabeth Kübler-Ross's groundbreaking work on the five stages of death and dying (1969). They have everything to do with the change process in schools. These stages can provide a guide for instructional leaders as they support faculty through emotions which they may not understand or anticipate. Consider what her five stages sound like in a school change process:

Denial: It's just a fad, another passing phase. I'm just going to stay below the radar for this year, they'll transfer the principal, and we'll just pretend this never happened.

Anger: Whose brainstorm was this stupid idea? I'm going to call my union rep, my neighbor the school board member, and the local newspaper. I'm going to plan an uprising so large they will be sorry they ever came up with this idea.

Bargaining: What if we start the new textbook adoption two years from now? There has been a lot going on this year, and next year we are renovating the cafeteria. How about two years from now?

Depression: I used to love teaching. Maybe I am just too old. Maybe I should see a doctor. I have been really exhausted and might have anemic blood levels. I need to call in sick. I am just not feeling well.

Acceptance: I know that the demographics in our community have dramatically changed since I first started to teach here. I honestly don't know how to teach the demographic majority of kids who now come to our school – students whose first language is not English. I want to learn how, so I can be a better teacher for my kids.

The role of an instructional leader is to listen carefully for evidence that suggests which stage a teacher might be navigating through. When they are denying, your job is to remind them that this is real and they can do it. When they are angry, you read between the lines, practice dispassionate disengagement, and hear their rage as masked panic and fear. When they try to bargain, there is no bargaining but lots of choices they can make in how to be supported, so that they can experience success. When they seem depressed, spend time listening to their concerns and team them up with a buddy to share positive experiences with the new initiative. When they arrive at acceptance, invite them to reflect on the process and lessons learned that they can borrow for next time.

THE IMPLEMENTATION DIP

In *Leading in a Culture of Change* (2001) Michael Fullan proposes the concept of "implementation dip", which anticipates a drop in performance and confidence in every person who goes through real change (*Figure 1*).

Figure 1. Implementation dip (Fullan, 2001)

There are critical junctures in the implementation dip. The first is when a change event has occurred, and life as we know it has ended. It can range from a death of someone important to you to "I just heard that I have to teach the second grade next year and I never taught the second grade before". The change is real and it kicks off the second aspect of this model, which is known as "the descent". You leave the safety of what was known and descend into the great abyss of the unknown (e.g., using a new math textbook, teaching in a new room down the hall away from your friends, or reporting to a new evaluator). A wise instructional leader will take the time to observe and study the behavior of exactly how their teachers descend... angrily, quietly, diplomatically, or refusing to move at all. I am reminded of an exceptionally skilled teacher colleague, who, when told that she would be reporting to a new sub school principal, actually parked herself in the trophy case in the hallway holding a sign which read "Hell No! I won't GO!". She was parked there for three days, until ultimately she came out, and reported to the new evaluator.

This descent correlates with my theory of behavioral response, which I call the "grace continuum" (*Figure 2*).

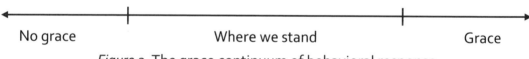

Figure 2. The grace continuum of behavioral response

It is important for you as instructional leader to note how much grace each individual is bringing to the descent, from none (zero on the far left of the continuum, like my colleague in the trophy case) to the great grace of acceptance, which sounds like, "What do I need to do for myself to stay grounded and practice some self-care strategies when my world goes upside down for a while?" (at the opposite end, on the far right of the continuum). Usually, we fall somewhere in between. There is always a subtext as to why we fall where we fall on the continuum. To raise the collective wisdom and level of grace among the faculty we are to observe and reflect on our own progress through the descent. Encourage the faculty to practice the strategies of support and resourcefulness as they move into the unsettled space of descent.

The next critical juncture is when we hit rock bottom of the implementation dip. The descent has ended. We are no longer looking over our shoulder wishing for the good old days. We are just sitting there, sometimes depressed, sometimes shell shocked, sometimes racing to get out of that space. That is where your instructional leadership wisdom must kick in. You don't want teams running away from that place because it is the most creative, visionary part of the process. Ask the team to brainstorm what the new norms should be to support this new change. How do we want it to work? How do we want to interact together to support this new work? What resources and support would be helpful? Design the new world order! That can't happen if people are afraid to sit, be still, think, and dream.

When teams actually embrace this visionary work, it becomes the ticket for the last juncture in the process, known as the "re-ascent". It is through the development of the new norms, collaborations, and experimentations with new models and resources that the teams are lifted to far greater heights than before this new initiative even began. This ultimately makes the whole process worthwhile, because people are functioning at a much higher capacity level. They know how to navigate through change with greater grace for the next time, because there will always be a next time.

PLANNING FOR RESISTANCE

Knowing human nature, every instructional leader should anticipate, plan for, and strategically respond to different forms of resistance. Change challenges the status quo, our patterns and routines, what we are comfortable with. Because resistance is so predictable, and the building of your repertoire of responses is so strategically complex, the topic of resistance requires a chapter unto itself. Chapter 14 identifies these forms of resistance and discusses a series of strategic responses to support people through the roadblocks which they create for themselves and for others.

Building Your Instructional Leadership

WHAT LEADERSHIP FOR FACILITATING CHANGE LOOKS LIKE

As an instructional leader you should:

1. *proactively teach* the faculty about the change process and what we as a staff look like when we navigate through it.

2. *monitor* the faculty for "initiative fatigue" before introducing an additional major change.

3. *incorporate* new ideas purposefully, because they align with and support the mission and vision.

4. *support a culture* of change by creating a culture of producing the capacity to address the change.

5. *diagnose* the obstacles to change that individuals might experience and differentiate your responses of support to specifically address the identified obstacle.

6. *practice dispassionate disengagement*. Furious reactions are not aimed at you personally. See through the rage and keep your cool.

7. *pause to reflect*. When "the descent" stage of the implementation dip gains momentum and the staff are feeling overwhelmed, use it as a time to pause and reflect. Reflect on what has been accomplished, taking stock of the great work done so far.

8. *support the process*. Leaders need to take an active role within teams, saying "what can I do to help" and rolling up the sleeves to go through the mud with your faculty. Whether joining teams for meetings, providing additional resources, or being that perennial cheerleader, school leaders play a crucial role when teams navigate through change.

9. *embrace the six practices* that keep change moving in a positive direction, as described by Harvard Business School Professor Rosabeth Moss Kanter[1]: show up, speak up, look up, team up, never give up, and lift others up.

10. *stay grounded* as you assist others by collaborating with a confidential colleague or coach. Eat healthy food and get exercise to rid yourself of the stress and toxins that the faculty might project onto you. Remind yourself that the turmoil of the moment will pass, and there will be better days.

---

[1] see her talk "Six Keys to Leading Positive Change" at: https://www.youtube.com/watch?v=0wU5aTNPJbs

STRATEGIES FOR DEVELOPING GRACE AND REFLECTION WHILE NAVIGATING THROUGH CHANGE

1. Study the implementation dip model as a team or department. Think about the time when you experienced significant change, either personally or professionally, and discuss how you responded through each of those critical junctures. What did you learn from that experience? What would you want to become better at? Create a change goal for yourself in response.

2. Consider the five stages of Elizabeth Kübler-Ross (1969) and draw parallels between a significant change you experienced. How did each of those stages manifest themselves? With this hindsight in mind, what can you do to provide better support for yourself next time?

3. Dive into the research of why this change is important and valuable.

4. Find other schools or colleagues who are on the other side of this change and talk with them about their process and lessons learned.

5. Get smarter about the program or initiative to lower the anxiety.

6. Think about drawing on humor to assist your team through change. Watch the *New Yorker* cartoonist Liza Donnelly's TED talk entitled "Drawing on Humor for Change"[2] to shift the conversation and gain some perspective and empowerment.

7. Play "The Change Game"[3] to engage in exercises that teach the concept of change in a non-threatening way.

8. Discuss the following questions, which help to keep the team focused (Senge, 1999, p. 166):
   - Why is this change urgent?
   - Who wants it to happen?
   - What results do we want to produce?
   - How will we change?
   - Who will be involved?
   - Where is our support?
   - What do I personally have to do?

9. Take time to paint a picture of what successful implementation of the change will look like. Be detailed and specific. Then plan backward by doing a step-by-step task analysis. What will be the blueprint for achieving the change by intent, not by accident?

10. There are three big reasons why people change: they have learned a lot, they have suffered enough, or they got tired of always doing the same thing. Have a team discussion reflecting on their own experiences in response to these three categories. How do they connect with the initiatives at school?

---

2 available at: http://www.ted.com/talks/liza_donnelly_drawing_upon_humor_for_change
3 available at: https://www.isixsigma.com/training/training-materials-aids/change-game-engaging-exercisesteach-change/

BIBLIOGRAPHY

Barth, R. S. (2001). *Learning by Heart*. San Francisco, CA: Jossey-Bass.

Burke, W. W. (2002). *Organizational Xchange: Theory and Practice*. Thousand Oaks, CA: Sage Publications.

Deutschman, A. (2005). Change or Die. *Fast Company*, (94), 52–62. Retrieved from www.fastcompany.com/magazine/94/open_change_or_die.html 2005

DuFour, R. (2004). What is a "professional learning community"? *Educational Leadership*, 61(8), 1–6.

Evans, R. (1996). *The Human Side of School Change: Reform, Resistance, and the Real-Life Problems of Innovation*. San Francisco, CA: Jossey-Bass.

Ferguson, M. (1980). *The Aquarian Conspiracy: Personal and Social Transformation in Our Time*. Los Angeles, CA: J.P. Tarcher, Inc.

Fullan, M. (2001). *Leading in a Culture of Change*. San Francisco, CA: Jossey-Bass.

Fullan, M. (2011). *Change Leader: Learning to Do What Matters Most*. San Francisco, CA: Jossey-Bass.

Garmston, R., & B. Wellman (2013). *The Adaptive School: A Sourcebook for Collaborative Groups* (2nd ed.). Plymouth: Rowan and Littlefield Publishers.

Gleick, J. (1987). *Chaos: Making a New Science*, New York, NY: Viking Penguin.

Hall, G. E., & Hord, S. M. (2006). *Implementing Change: Patterns, Principles, and Potholes*. Boston, MA: Pearson/Allyn & Bacon.

Kübler-Ross, E. (1969). *On Death and Dying*. New York, NY: Macmillan.

Love, N. (2008). *Using Data to Improve Learning for All: A Collaborative Inquiry Approach*. Thousand Oaks, CA: Corwin.

Ogden, E. H., & Germinaro, V. (1995). *The Nation's Best Schools: Blueprint for Excellence* (Vol. 2). Lancaster, PA: Technomic.

Senge, P. M. (1999). *The Dance of Change: The Challenges of Sustaining Momentum in Learning Organizations*. New York, NY: Currency/Doubleday.

Senge, P. M. (2006). *The Fifth Discipline: The Art and Practice of the Learning Organization* (revised ed.). New York, NY: Doubleday.

Smith, L. (2008). *Schools That Change: Evidence-Based Improvement and Effective Change Leadership*. Thousand Oaks, CA: Corwin.

Sweeney, L., & Meadows, D. (1995). *The Systems Thinking Playbook*. White River Junction, VT: Chelsea Green Publishing.

Vygotsky, L. S. (1978). *Mind in Society: The Development of Higher Psychological Processes*. Cambridge, MA: Harvard University Press.

Building Your Conference Skill Repertoire

HOW TO USE CONVERSATION TO LEARN AND GROW
THE DRAMA OF THE SUBTEXT
A CONTINUUM OF LEARNING-FOCUSED INTERACTIONS
CALIBRATING CONVERSATIONS
DIFFICULT CONFERENCES
CONSCIOUSNESS OF OUR LANGUAGE AND SPEAKING CHOICES

> *Our conversations invent us. Through our speech and our silence, we become smaller or larger selves. Through our speech and our silence, we diminish or enhance the other person, and we narrow or expand the possibilities between us. How we use our voice detemines the quality of our relationships, who we are in the world, and what the world can be and might become. Clearly, a lot is at stake here.*
>
> Harriet Lerner,
> *The Dance of Connection* (2009)

Instructional leaders should encourage and welcome every conversation with their teachers to reflect on their skills and grow their capacity to expand student learning and achievement. The ultimate goal – higher-level achievement – correlates with the instructional choices their teachers make. Instructional conversations are critical for supporting teacher growth, and yet there are many individual and organizational obstacles to having an informed and fruitful conversation, such as poor time management or motivation, poor observational skills, or lack of collaborative structures and supportive school culture.

Instructional leaders should be motivated, disciplined, and skilled in time management to leave the office and spend most of their time observing and doing instructional rounds and walkthroughs to have a finger on the pulse of what is happening in every classroom.

They also need to be skilled in observing and collecting data (see Chapter 9, Observing for Learning).

Collaborative structures de-privatize teacher behavior, break down silos, and make teaching public, so that everyone can engage in instructional conversations with each other.

Similarly, the school culture should be such that focuses on continuous learning, reflection, and conversations about the craft of teaching and learning in the best interest of student achievement.

Last but not least, every meaningful conversation should rest on the foundations of a psychologically safe and trusting environment (see Chapters 1–3).

In addition to these structural and organizational obstacles, a large obstacle is how teachers receive and internalize the feedback and conversations they are a part of.

HOW TO USE CONVERSATION TO LEARN AND GROW

According to Harvard Law School professor Sheila Heen, the receiver of information is in the driver's seat in terms of what information they will take in and whether they choose to act on it and change or not (Stone & Heen, 2014)[1]. Receiving feedback is a skill that needs to be named, contextualized, supported by the culture of the school, and practiced with a clear set of guidelines.

In strong school cultures that celebrate continuous learning, teachers and administrators are actively seeking feedback, reflective conferences, and hones data-driven conversations, which focus on what is negative, so that they can make a product or process better. The touchy-feely-looks-great comments are useless. They look for the flaws to go from good to great. This reminds me of a high-school biology teacher who was exceptionally skilled. His brand new science supervisor observed him and told him how inspiring he was, how his use of technology was cutting-edge, how his depth of content knowledge and pedagogical skill were preeminent. The

---

[1] watch her TEDTalk " How to Use Others' Feedback to Learn and Grow" at: https://www.youtube.com/watch?v=FQNbaKkYk_Q

science teacher then proceeded to demean the science supervisor for his lack of supervisory skill. He said, "I know I am fabulous. I know I do all those things. You didn't provide a single thing for me to work on, to think about, to investigate further. What kind of supervisor are you?" Research suggests that people who solicit negative feedback have higher work satisfaction, adapt more quickly, and experience higher levels of success. It changes how others see you and experience you in your work environment.

Think about the coaching you received and rejected. Why didn't you take it? Perhaps you didn't respect the person with whom you were having the conversation and didn't care about what they had to share. Perhaps the coach wasn't skilled to coach and ended up giving you advice you didn't ask for. Perhaps there was no trust between you.

Even if the instructional leader knows how to lead reflective conversations and share feedback, it still doesn't mean that the teachers will change their practice. What it will do is increase the odds that teachers will truly reflect upon the feedback and discussion, and then decide how it may or may not be incorporated in their practice.

THE DRAMA OF THE SUBTEXT

One of the reasons why instructional leaders hesitate to have calibrating conversations or share problem information is the apprehension of the teacher's response. University of Pennsylvania psychology professor Martin Seligman finds that 50% of a teacher's response is their pre-wiring that comes from a very deep subtext (the submerged part of the iceberg), 40% is the story that the teacher creates from their hard-wired response to what they heard, and only 10% comes from the data shared (2006).

In response, teachers could question the truth in the data or the experience of the administrator involved in the conversation. Some of them could be extremely sensitive. Seligman says that the range from insensitive to highly sensitive can be as much as 3000%. The recovery with highly sensitive people could actually take years. "You need a thicker skin" does not help in this situation.

Insensitive people provide a different set of challenges: They may not realize that they are part of a reflective dialogue or that they are expected to connect the feedback to their own craft. As a result, a skilled instructional leader will develop with this teacher an action plan of next steps which are expected to be addressed, and follow up conversation will be a part of the plan.

A CONTINUUM OF LEARNING-FOCUSED INTERACTIONS

Bruce Wellman and Laura Lipton in their book *Learning Focused Supervision* (2013) designed a continuum to address four categories of conferencing skills. These categories include coaching (see Chapter 10), collaborating (see Chapter 3), consulting (providing expertise and resources to address a specific issue), and

Building Your Instructional Leadership

calibrating (see below).

This third section of *Building Your Instructional Leadership* focuses on the situational complexities which instructional leaders confront. This chapter highlights the complexity of situations in which you have to provide information that may be difficult to hear and receive, name instruction which is not good enough and needs improvement, or name gaps to be formalized and make part of improvement plans. The conference structure and the conversation are calibrating ones. I shall also focus on the steps to having a calibrating conversation and the underpinnings of having difficult conversations.

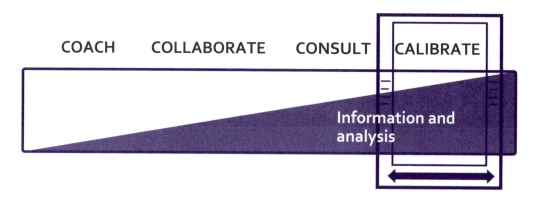

Figure 1. Continuum of learning-focused interaction (Lipton & Wellman, 2013)

CALIBRATING CONVERSATIONS

An instructional leader will choose to have a calibrating conversation when the teacher has not made progress with her/his skill set or the students have not made progress in learning even after coaching, collaborating, and consulting. The calibrating conference is used as the last resort. The idea is to repeat clearly and unequivocally the targets to be achieved and the criteria by which achievement (success) is measured and then to compare these with the information about the current level of students' skills/learning. The critical point of a calibrating conference is drawing the teacher's attention to the gap between the two. The discussion that ensues should address the instructional strategies and dispositions required to close that gap.

The teaching models, exemplars, and expectations become the "third point", which guides the conversation. The third point is defined as any information that specifies an area to reflect on. In a calibrating conversation, the third point could be the preestablished criteria for what constitutes effective instruction. The third point could also be the information about current student learning (student work samples, grade distributions, or the number of students who have requested transfer from the teacher's class). Having the third point helps, as it keeps the conversation on the track of expectations and performance data. It is cognitive, as opposed to affective and personal.

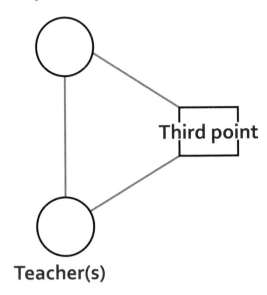

Figure 2. The "third point" as the point of reference in conversation (Garmston & Wellman, 2013; Lipton & Wellman, 2013)

DIFFICULT CONFERENCES

A skilled instructional leader will reframe a difficult conversation into an opportunity to learn and grow. Do not look at it as a stumbling block or a "gotcha" moment. You should seek to understand the teacher's thinking behind the pattern of ineffective decisions that have led to this point and what is specifically important to the teacher in terms of their professional growth. You will seek ways to build bridges to new ideas that have some link to the old ideas.

Preparation steps for the conference

1. As you prepare for the conference, you should first get your facts right:
2. check what the required level of teaching performance is;
3. identify the standards which student performance does not meet;
4. get data from multiple sources to diagnose the problem (remember data triangulation from the social studies?). Having more than one source makes your point valid. It is not a fluke. You identify a pattern that is supported by several pieces of evidence; and
5. use these data to identify the gap between the current and required performance.

Be ready to describe the gap which exists between the present level of teaching and the desired outcome for student learning.

Then prepare yourself mentally. Remind yourself that you are advocating for students and their learning. If learning fails based on the chronic lack of teaching skill, you must address it.

Imagine that you are leading this conversation with "dispassionate disengagement". This means that you are pretending that you are a reporter on the scene. You are not a player in the scene. This is a critical shift to remember, which will keep your personal emotions separate and distinct from this conversation.

Design a mental platform to stand on. Instructional leaders know that they can only control their own thinking and responses. They have no control over how the other person will respond. It would therefore be inappropriate to measure the success of this conference based on whether it has made the teacher embrace a different attitude or alter practice. That may never happen. What you can measure is whether you met your own personal goals. If you have a short fuse, perhaps your goal is to stay dispassionately disengaged, no matter how many times the teacher tries to get you emotionally involved or angry. Perhaps your goal is to stay on message and stick to the data, no matter how many times the teacher tries to change the subject or make excuses. What you don't ever want to happen is to have a drive home after the conference kicking yourself because you took the bait, got defensive or angry, and lost your cool. This is how you loose your credibility and the purpose of the conversation. Your personal goals keep you grounded and separate from the data. This is why you should define them before you ever begin the conversation.

Then compose "Students need..." statements (desired outcome) based on the data that you have collected and analyzed.

CONSCIOUSNESS OF OUR LANGUAGE AND SPEAKING CHOICES

Robert Kegan and Lisa Laskow Lahey have researched how the way we talk mirrors the way we think (2002). They recommend seven transformations or deliberate reflective stances that we want to pursue in difficult conversations with our faculty. These seven transformations are as follows:

1. *from the language of complaint to the language of commitment.* While this may seem pretty straightforward, the idea is to reframe a complaint as a sign that the teacher cares. By acknowledging a complaint, you can turn it into a teacher's commitment to improve.

2. *from the language of blame to the language of personal responsibility.* Commitment is still the key word. The point is not to land blame but to establish with the teacher which part of underperformance belongs to the teacher, which part is of her or his own making and therefore of largest influence. This is the room for improvement.

3. *from the language of New Year's resolutions to the language of competing commitments.* Everyone knows that few people follow through their easily declared promises of commitment. Once you've established personal responsibility, see what other teacher's commitment stands in the way. It may be a commitment to an assumption that undermines the declared commitment, a fear of being perceived incompetent, of failing, or the need to be liked by everyone, but once it is out in the open, the two of you can work something out

or at least be aware of it.

4. *from the language of big assumptions that hold us to the language of assumptions we individually hold.* This transformation is all about taking assumptions for what they are—assumptions. Not absolute truths. Begin a difficult conversation aware that the data you've collected and the conclusions you've drawn are but assumptions and perceptions only. There is doubt, the need for inquiry, questioning, and dialogue to seek to understand. You are offering propositions and wonderings which need to be checked out for their validity.

5. *from the language of prizes and praising to the language of ongoing regard.* This transformation is a shift in focus from the person to the deeds. People tend to praise by assigning attributes (you're great, awesome, skillful, or the opposite) where it would more sincere and effective to acknowledge how someone's action affected you. Praise tends to wear off, sincere acknowledgments of someone's worthy actions never do.

6. *from the language of rules and policies to the language of public agreements.* This one has a lot to do with big assumptions and their deconstruction. The idea is to look beyond the rules and policies to make common ground that is acceptable for both.

7. *from the language of destructive and even constructive criticism to the language of deconstructive criticism.* In line with deconstructing big assumptions and rules, replace criticism, which could lead to an unproductive clash, with questions seeking to learn something new from the situation before you "teach and fix". Seek to change vantage points. Seek to understand the theory of the other person. Seek to facilitate an interchange of "reciprocal learning".

What does it mean in practice? In difficult conversations complaining, blame, assumptions, and criticism are bound to happen, and when they do, transform them into opportunities to reframe the conversation. To look through or past complaints, blame, and assumptions. Instead of complaints about students not learning, talk about how committed you and your teacher are to make sure that they do learn. Instead of blaming the teacher or letting her/him blame others for the lack of student progress, shift the conversation to personal responsibility and what competing commitment stands in the way.

With these transformative opportunities in mind, you, the instructional leader, are playing a constant game of mental chess during the conference, listening carefully for the language to transform and get the conversation back to the intended course, and closer to behavioral change, with the only purpose to improve student achievement.

Building Your Instructional Leadership

WHAT LEADERSHIP FOR CALIBRATION LOOKS LIKE

As an instructional leaders you should:

1. always refer to the third point, withholding your judgment and opinion.
2. take the "I" out of the conversation. It is not about the persons involved in it. The focus should be on the students and their learning.
3. seek to coach, collaborate, and consult.
4. use calibrating and difficult conversations as the last resort and only after you establish clear pattern in poor practice and student performance.
5. clarify what are non-negotiables in terms of instructional expectations, and communicate them consistently.
6. define problems and required actions verbally and in writing. Revisit them as the third point.
7. name the expected criteria for instructional success.
8. establish timelines for addressing the gaps identified in the conference.
9. offer support throughout the process.
10. model professionalism and positive relationship-building with the teachers, regardless of their behavior.

STRATEGIES FOR SUCCESSFUL CALIBRATING AND DIFFICULT CONFERENCES

1. Identify your own Achilles heel that might get in the way of conducting a difficult conversation, such as the need that everyone likes you or that you don't like conflict, and be conscious of it so you can manage it.

2. Run a mental scenario in your mind imagining what the teacher could bring to the conference to sabotage it. Plan how you would respond to different scenarios.

3. Design criteria for your own performance that is separate and distinct from how the teacher might respond. Reflect on how well you did when the conference is over.

4. Practice "reporter on the scene" or "broken record" strategies (repeating in monotone fashion the expectations, regardless of all of the backtalk and excuses which may come your way) as a way to foster dispassionate disengagement.

5. Improve your skills in active listening and probing for specificity.

6. Stay focused to keep the conversation on the message and to clearly state what you expect to see.

7. Facilitate problem-solving to come up with a plan of action.

8. Watch instructional coach Lucy West's video about principal-to-teacher conference skills[2]. Consider how you incorporate these skills into your repertoire.

9. Do a mock conference with a colleague and have her/him play the teacher, so that you can prepare for your worst-case scenario.

10. Practice mindfulness and meditation before the actual conference, so that you can stay centered and focused during it.

---

[2] available at: https://www.youtube.com/watch?v=Sp4yqH5E8pQ

BIBLIOGRAPHY

Lerner, H. (2009). *The Dance of Connection*. New York, NY: HarperCollins.

Lipton, L. & Wellman, B. (2013). *Learning-Focused Supervision: Developing Professional Expertise in Standards-Driven Systems*. Arlington, MA: MiraVia.

Garmston, R., & B. Wellman (2013). *The Adaptive School: A Sourcebook for Collaborative Groups* (2nd ed.). Plymouth: Rowan and Littlefield Publishers.

Kegan, R., & Laskow Lahey, L. (2002). *How the Way We Talk Can Change the Way We Work: Seven Languages for Transformation*. San Francisco, CA: Jossey-Bass.

Seligman, M. E. P. (2006). *Learned Optimism: How to Change your Mind and Your Life*. New York, NY: Vintage Books.

Stone, D., & Heen, S. (2014). *Thanks for the Feedback: The Science and Art of Receiving Feedback Well*. New York, NY: Viking.

Dealing with Difficult People, Situations, and Conversations

CRUCIAL CONFRONTATIONS

THROWING DIFFICULT PEOPLE AND PERSONALITIES INTO THE MIX

PLAYING TACTICAL CHESS IN DIFFICULT SITUATIONS

REDIRECTING TOXIC WORDS AND EMOTIONS

> "*Education either functions as an instrument which is used to facilitate integration of the younger generation into the logic of the present system and bring about conformity to it, or it becomes "the practice of freedom", the means by which men and women deal critically and creatively with reality and discover how to participate in the transformation of their world.*"
>
> Patterson, Grenny, McMillan & Switzler,
> *Crucial Confrotations* (2005, pp. 4–5)

CRUCIAL CONFRONTATIONS

After 10,000 hours of studying leaders, Patterson, Grenny, McMillan, and Switzler, the authors of Crucial Confrontations, found that what set influential leaders apart from all others wasn't technical skill, title, or charisma. It was their ability to hold people accountable while maintaining a relationship. They created an invitational atmosphere for people to speak up and share concerns (see Chapter 1—Building Psychological Safety). They also addressed the need to talk face to face about an important issue. They purposely didn't confront through the use of email, understanding that email can lead to even more problems based on the potential misinterpretation of every word and the implied tone behind them. Their handling of crucial confrontations was based on learned skill, not the implementation of a policy (2005).

When preparing for a confrontation, make sure that you are preparing for the real issue. You note the pattern that keeps repeating over time. Then you discuss the effect of this pattern on the relationships with the people on the receiving end of this problematic pattern or behavior. A true leader is someone who prefers the risks of speaking up over the certainty of silence and the problem perpetuating itself. True leaders listen to their conscience and they take action.

THROWING DIFFICULT PEOPLE AND PERSONALITIES INTO THE MIX

One of the things that makes working in schools and school systems endlessly fascinating is the multitude of personalities which are all floating around and working together under one roof and one mission and vision of the school. According to Robert Bramson (*Coping With Difficult People*, 1981), you can confront the hostile aggressive, the complainer, the silent unresponsive, the super-agreeable, the negativist, the know-it-all, and the indecisive faculty member. Imagine if you have one of each in a department. Even so, the structure for confronting broken promises, unmet expectations, and missed deadlines remains the same. You name the expectation, lay evidence of the problem, and point out the gap. The conversation is focused on how to close the gap and next steps to take. In addition, the instructional leader will add the additional skill of thinking strategically and playing a good game of mental, tactical chess. These different personalities become pieces on your chessboard.

PLAYING TACTICAL CHESS IN DIFFICULT SITUATIONS

On average (with standard deviations), 5% of your faculty is made up of omnivores. Bramson would call them the "super-agreeables". They love everything. They are your cheerleaders and biggest supporters. When you are depressed you visit their classroom to feel better. When you need people to sign up for the committee, they readily agree, whether they know what the committee's purpose is or not. They bring great enthusiasm, energy, and happiness to every task they take on. A strategic leader knows that this five percent of the population has the least amount of credibility with the rest of the faculty, because they love everything. Their enthusiasm can get on people's nerves. They are seen as "principal's pets".

A skilled strategist realizes that the power in shifting a culture, embracing an initiative, and getting everyone moving in the right direction lies with the "skeptics", who make 15% of the population. A leader will not get defensive when the skeptic demands to know what is behind a conversation, a change, the issue at hand. What the implications are. How much will it really cost in terms of time, resources, and personal inconvenience. A leader calmly appreciates these questions and answers them readily. Then a miracle occurs. The skeptics have their concerns answered, and there is dialogue. Then they turn into omnivore-likes. They are bought in, and see themselves as a leader with the next steps moving forward.

Now the instructional leader has 20% of the population. Malcolm Gladwell in his book *The Tipping Point* (2000) says that 20% is all you need to get things moving in the right direction.

The next critical juncture is what happens with the "passive consumers", who account for 60% of the faculty population. Passive consumers are dead weight. They take up space. They could lean positive or they could lean negative, depending on how the leader structures the situation. This is where the skeptics come in particularly handy. Because they have the greatest amount of credibility, each skeptic becomes a "team leader". One omnivore and 5-6 passive consumers are all under the leadership of a skeptic, who leads the way in support of the school vision. With passive consumers now leaning positive, you've got 80% of the population moving forward from slightly positive to downright ecstatic.

Then there are still the 15% of the faculty who are deemed "negative". They are now surrounded and neutralized, with no place for their negativity to go. It is like surrounding an oil spill. They are dispersed among the teams led by the skeptics, who are acting like omnivores. They start getting on with the program, or at least they become quiet. This leaves the remaining 5%, whom we shall call "saboteurs".

Saboteurs can be passive aggressive, smiling to your face, pledging total agreement, and then undermining you at every chance. They will have no intention of supporting a request or initiative. They will manipulatively seek to undermine, while enacting enthusiastic support. The good news is that they only represent 5% of the population and don't have any place to go, given that 95% is marching to the correct beat. That is where two strategies come into play.

The first strategy to use when working with saboteurs is "Better to keep the camel in the tent than outside of the tent." Outside of the tent, the camel is left to its own devices, which includes knocking the tent down. Keeping the camel inside your tent means that they become your new best friend. Your eye is on them, and they are totally uncomfortable. Maybe their discomfort leads them to find other positions in other systems, which is just fine. The second strategy is "Play Wayne Gretzky". For those of you who may not be familiar with Wayne Gretzky, he is considered to be the greatest ice hockey player of all times. One of the things that makes his brilliance surpass all other players is the mental game he plays. He analyzes where he believes the puck will go before it actually arrives at its destination. He skates to the place of his prediction, waits for the puck, and hits it to the next place. As an instructional leader, you are invited to morph yourself into a version of Wayne Gretzky. Analyze where you believe the saboteur will go and get there first. Get to the union president first. Review the contract loopholes first. Inform and educate the school board first. That way, when the puck gets there, it is old news. It takes the air right out of the saboteur. You never confront a passive aggressive head on. Just skate to where the puck will go, and leave them in the ice spray.

REDIRECTING TOXIC WORDS AND EMOTIONS

In Better Conversations (2016) Jim Knight advises instructional leaders to hone the skill of controlling their emotions: When we fail to control our emotions we fail to hear what needs to be heard. He offers a three-step strategy to help with that task:

Name it: Identify situations where your buttons might be pushed and what is the root of your anger.

Reframe it: Change how you feel about emotionally difficult conversations by adopting a new way of looking at them. See yourself as a listener, learner, game player, or detached observer. Remind yourself that you are a listener. It is not your job to point out to someone something you think he or she may be missing. In Chapter 13, I discussed the skills of "dispassionate disengagement" and playing "reporter on the scene" as additional ways to support this concept of "reframing". William Ury, author of *Getting Past No: Negotiating with Difficult People* (1991), calls the detachment skill "going to the balcony". The balcony is a metaphor for a mental attitude of detachment. From the balcony you can calmly evaluate the conflict almost as if you were a third party. You can think constructively for both sides and look for a mutually satisfactory way to resolve the problem. Personally, I follow the "24-hour rule" to cool down if I don't trust my control of emotions at some point.

Tame it: Ury (1991) offers a number of strategies to tame emotions: pausing (the first norm of collaboration listed in Chapter 3), counting to ten, and breathing deeply. Be quick to hear, slow to speak, and slow to act. He reminds us to paraphrase and check if we heard correctly. He tells us to break vicious cycles and stop proving each other wrong, because there is no way out (*Figure 1*).

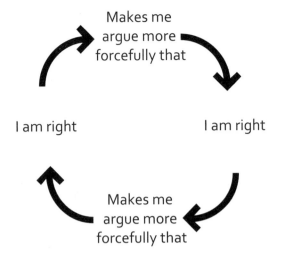

Figure 1. Vicious cycle in conversations (Knight, 2016, p. 165)

Stone, Patton, Heen & Fisher (2000) remind us to change the conversation when it gets caught in an unproductive cycle. You can say something like, "It wasn't my intent for us to have a problem. Instead of getting more frustrated, let's work together to find a solution". Kegan & Laskow Lahey remind us to stop working from assumptions (see Chapter 13). Ruiz (2001) believes that the problem with making assumptions about what others are thinking is that we believe these assumptions are the truth. We make these assumptions about what others are doing or thinking and then we blame them and react. Eventually we end up misunderstanding, taking it personally, and creating a big drama for nothing (pp. 63–64).

Another way to redirect toxic conversations is by never letting them begin in the first place. When a new high school principal was transferred to a school where I taught, he gave an opening speech which remains emblazoned in my mind all these decades later. With his heavy Texan twang, he lectured and threatened us with never wanting to hear a word of gossip about anyone by anyone who is a member of this faculty. Instead, he demanded, we were to refer to each other as "a mighty fine person" no matter what we might think of each other. Of course, we had to tease each other in the hallway after the opening meeting, introducing each other as a "mighty fine person", but the message hit home. If you can't say something nice, don't say anything at all. Gossip can destroy the culture of a school by its toxicity. Kolb & Williams (2000) offer a proactive set of team norms and tactics to keep everyone conscious of this important task (*Table 1*).

Tactic	What is it?	Example
Interrupting	Anticipating a negative conversation and changing the topic before it begins	"I forgot that I am doublebooked. I am so sorry, but we need to reschedule."
Naming	Labeling what is happening so it becomes clearer for everyone to observe	"If we keep whining about the students, we are not going to come up with some useful solutions."
Correcting	Clarifying a statement that is not accurate	"I was at the meeting, and the team was actually opposed to the idea."
Diverting	Moving the conversation in different direction	"Speaking of the math program, when are they going to start their new textbook adoption process?"

Table 1. Modified from Tactics to redirect unhealthy conversations (adapted from Knight, 2016, p. 175)

Instructional leaders may also make use of some of the Toltec wisdom when they work with their staff. Summing this wisdom up, this is what David Ruiz asks us to do in his *Four Agreements* (2001):

1. Be impeccable with your words.
2. Don't take anything personally.
3. Don't make assumptions
4. Always do your best.

If the faculty truly embraces these behaviors, difficult situations disappear.

Chapter 14 / Dealing with Difficult People, Situations, and Conversations

WHAT LEADERSHIP IN DIFFICULT SITUATIONS LOOKS LIKE

1. Don't lose your cool. Remind yourself to practice the Name It—Reframe It—Tame It strategy.

2. Listen carefully to what is important to the difficult person. Use those ideas as a way to negotiate the best alternative to a negotiated agreement (aka BATNA) on the direction where your school is going.

3. Always model respect and courtesy, even if the person with whom you are interacting is inappropriate and disrespectful.

4. Enact Daniel Pink's ABCs Of Leadership (from *To Sell Is Human*, 2012): *attunement* (seek to understand where the resistance is coming from), *buoyancy* (don't take anything personally), and *clarity* (state what you need and expect clearly in a sound bite).

5. Tack with the wind. Do not take an aggressive person head on. Follow their line of thinking by listening and inquiring for as long as possible.

6. Keep the camel in the tent with your most damaging saboteurs.

7. With clear expectations, keep up the heat with people who are not modeling what is best for students in your school.

8. Brush up on your tactical chess game. There is a reason why world chess master Bobby Fischer stared at his chess board for two years before making a move. He was thinking through the implications and total board reaction in response to each and every move and consciously selected which implications were the best for winning the game in the long run. You don't have the luxury of two years, but the process of strategic thinking is exactly the same.

9. Remember your values and let your conscience be your guide behind every difficult discussion and decision.

10. Stay focused and flexible when others try to intimidate, cry, or sulk.

Building Your Instructional Leadership

STRATEGIES FOR SUCCESSFUL NAVIGATION THROUGH DIFFICULT SITUATIONS AND PERSONALITIES

Consider strengthening your skillset when responding in toxic situations using Jim Knight's online templates accompanying his *Better Conversations* (2016)[1]:

1. looking *back* on controlling your toxic emotions.
2. looking *at* controlling your toxic emotions (part 1 of 2).
3. looking *at* controlling your toxic emotions (part 2 of 2).
4. getting proactive by looking *ahead*: controlling your toxic emotions.
5. managing your emotions and gaining the upper hand by redirecting toxic conversations.
6. Role-play and practice a crucial confrontation before you initiate the actual one.
7. Find the courage to ask for help in thinking through the specific issue, in getting another set of eyes for the data, in analyzing the implications.
8. Practice reframing from what's wrong with them to what is going on with them (Stone et al., 2000):
   - reframe truth as a possible story or perspective;
   - reframe accusations as intentions;
   - reframe blame as contribution; and
   - reframe judgment as feeling.
9. Prepare, prepare, prepare... by doing your homework, making sure the confrontation is worthy of addressing, clarifying the problem; analyzing implications, and exploring all sides and perspectives.
10. Practice framing inquiry questions and seeking to understand.

---

[1] available at: http://resources.corwin.com/KnightBetterConversations

BIBLIOGRAPHY

Bramson, R. M. (1981). *Coping with Difficult People*. New York, NY: Dell Publishing.

Gladwell, M. (2000). *The Tipping Point: How Little Things Can Make a Big Difference*. Boston, MA: Little, Brown.

Kegan, R., & Laskow Lahey, L. (2002). *How the Way We Talk Can Change the Way We Work: Seven Languages for Transformation*. San Francisco, CA: Jossey-Bass.

Knight, J. (2016). B*etter Conversations: Coaching Ourselves and Each Other to Be More Credible, Caring, and Connected*. Thousand Oaks, CA: Corwin Press.

Kolb, D. M., & Williams, J. (2000). *The Shadow Negotiaton: How Women Can Master the Hidden Agendas That Determine Bargaining Success*. New York, NY: Simon & Schuster.

Patterson, K., Grenny, J., McMillan, R., & Switzler, A. (2005). *Crucial Confrontations: Tools for Resolving Broken Promises, Violated Expectations, and Bad Behavior*. New York, NY: McGraw-Hill.

Pink, D. H. (2012). *To Sell Is Human: The Surprising Truth About Moving Others*. New York, NY: Riverhead Books.

Ruiz, D. M. (2001). *The Four Agreements: A Practical Guide to Personal Freedom (A Toltec Wisdom Book)*. San Rafael, CA: Amber-Allen Publishing.

Stone, D., Patton, B., Heen, S., & Fisher, R. (2000). *Difficult Conversations: How to Discuss What Matters Most*. New York, NY: Penguin.

Ury, W. (1991). *Getting Past No: Negotiating with Difficult People*. New York, NY: Bantam Books.

Building Your Own Resilience

THE BIG PICTURE
***B* IS FOR BUOYANCY**
SKILLS TO BUILD UP RESILIENCE
BUILDING YOUR OPTIMISM
THE LONELINESS OF LEADERSHIP
NURTURING OUR EMOTIONAL WELLBEING
THE ROLE OF SPIRITUALITY
PRACTICE PERSEVERANCE
HOW ADAPTIVE ARE YOU?

15

" *A worker bee is just over a centimeter long and weighs only about sixty miligrams; nevertheless, she can fly with a load heavier than herself.* "

Sue Monk Kidd,
The Secret Life of Bees (2002)

THE BIG PICTURE

Evidence abounds that today's instructional leaders are operating in environments that generate more stress and strain than ever before. In a Connecticut statewide study (Sogunro, 2012) more than 96% of the instructional leaders claimed to have experienced work-related stress at a level that was affecting their mental and physical health, work habits, and productivity. Due to constant stress, many considered early retirement. Sogunro identified seven major stress factors: unpleasant relationships and conflicts, time constraints and related issues, school crises, challenging policy demands and overwhelming mandates, budgetary constraints and related issues, fear of failure, and negative publicity and dealing with media. These findings have enormous implications that call for learning and developing resilience skills, so that you can cope with the physical and emotional demands of your job.

How leaders react and deal with the mental and emotional assaults which come with the job looks very similar to Michael Fullan's "implementation dip" (2001) described in Chapter 12 – (Navigating Through Change). As soon as a new situation occurs – a media assault, parental attack, devastating budget cut, or union protest – the deteriorating phase kicks in, and the leader needs every resilience skill to rebound. These skills help the leader to adapt, recover, and grow. With limited or no resilience skills, the leader becomes stuck, depressed, and incapable of rising to the occasion. Patterson, Goens & Reed (2009) described the experiences of assistant superintendent Ray Denton of a Tennessee school district, who went through all the rebound stages, and asked him to sum up the lessons learned to help others grow in the face of adversity. This is what he said, "Number one: don't forget the politics. Number two, you're either going to be a light or you're going to shut light out. I would rather be a light. It doesn't always mean cracking a joke. It means someone who is going to be brightness for others. At times this may mean I need to lean on somebody else who is brighter than me that day, but there's got to be someone there holding the torch." (2009, p. 8)

B IS FOR BUOYANCY

Daniel Pink in his book *To Sell is Human* investigates how door-to-door Fuller brush salesmen stay in the game after enduring an ocean of rejection, wave after wave of rebuffs, refusals, and repudiations (2012, p. 99). Pink analyzes three strategies that keep the salesmen resilient and optimistic or "buoyant", to use his term.

The first strategy is "interrogative self-talk". Instead of pumping oneself up with big, broad affirmations of "I am all-powerful" or "I am successful", he found that posing a question was far more successful. He likens the question to the one that children's television character "Bob the Builder" is famous for asking: "Can we do it? Yes, we can!" The difference here is that it is not a positive or negative self-talk message, but a question. A question that inspires autonomous, intrinsic motivation to pursue a goal.

The second strategy is what Pink calls "positive ratios". This means making sure that the ratio of emotions is 3:1 in favor of the positive ones.

His last strategy to strengthen buoyancy is the use of "explanatory style'". Pink discusses Martin Seligman's research on learned optimism (see Chapter 13) and the term he coined, called "learned helplessness". He calls that a function of the

explanatory style. It is a form of self-talk that occurs after a challenging or stressful experience. Those who give up easily, who become helpless even in situations where they could do something, who see bad events as permanent, pervasive, and personal, those people model a negative, pessimistic explanatory style. It is debilitating, diminishes performance, triggers depression, turns setbacks into disaster, and sinks buoyancy and resilience on the job. Both Martin Seligman and Daniel Pink recommend "flexible optimism", which is optimism with open eyes.

To help us grow our resilience in the face of difficult circumstances, the famed author and Buddhist nun Pema Chödrön reminds us that Buddha taught three principal characteristics of human existence: impermanence, egolessness, and suffering or dissatisfaction (2001). To consciously build our resilience, we should remind ourselves that our jobs, our standing in the eyes of our supervisors, or the feedback we receive are all impermanent. We can't hang our soul and emotions on that. We also grow resilience by keeping our egos in check as often and as much as possible. Chödrön also reminds us not to be surprised or depressed when we suffer or are dissatisfied. Welcome to being alive! It is all part of the process and our journey on earth. These principles have the power to reframe circumstances and help us to rebound.

SKILLS TO BUILD UP RESILIENCE

When instructional leaders are under the stress of challenge and unfavorable odds, it is always good to remember that we have a choice. We can choose how we face these situations and what decisions we make. We build our capacity by strengthening our ethics, personal efficacy, and self-trust. Patterson, Goens & Reed remind us of our abilities to grow (2009, p. 10). These are:

- our ability to reason, make decisions, and assume responsibility for the actions we take;
- our ability to help others develop a sense of efficacy in doing their work and meeting obligations;
- our ability to adhere to the core principles and values in making decisions; we do not just sell out or do what is easy or expedient.

Resilience builds up by giving a realistic appraisal of what is happening now and what will be happening in the future. It grows when we draw from the well of our personal values, personal efficacy, personal wellbeing, and other people's support. It grows through perseverance to stay on course under fire. Finally, resilience is built by taking personal responsibility for the mistakes made and by correcting them.

Marianne Williamson reminds us of our resilience and capacity when she says, "Our deepest fear is not that we are inadequate. Our deepest fear is that we are powerful beyond measure. It is our light, not our darkness, that most frightens us. We ask ourselves, 'Who am I to be brilliant, gorgeous, talented, fabulous?' Actually, who are you not to be? You are a child of God. Your playing small does not serve the world.

There is nothing enlightened about shrinking so that other people won't feel insecure around you. We are all meant to shine, as children do. We were born to make manifest the glory of God that is within us. It is not just in some of us; it's in everyone. And as we let our own light shine, we unconsciously give others permission to do the same. As we are liberated from our own fear, our presence automatically liberates others."(*A Return to Love*, 1992, p. 190)

BUILDING YOUR OPTIMISM

Patterson & Kelleher (2005) discuss the importance of realistic optimism in the face of adversity, as opposed to the all-glowing "Suzy Sunshine" response when the Titanic is going down. They've found that realistic optimism leads to better social relationships, health, and flexibility in thinking. Optimists see adversity as a challenge, find solutions to problems, maintain confidence, and rebound after setbacks. As a result, optimists work harder and have a higher morale. They have a sense of hope. If you model realistic optimism as an instructional leader, all of these things will come to you as a result.

Resilient leadership is when we consciously build our own efficacy. We remind ourselves of our sense of purpose and our ability to trust ourselves and our leadership. This mindset breeds the sense of presence in the moment and a quiet confidence that gives courage to your faculty. It looks like humility. Resilient leaders believe in themselves, their ability to organize and to act in adverse situations. Think about Nelson Mandela, who was jailed on Robben Island for 27 years, or Martin Luther King leading peaceful marches for civil rights. They modeled authenticity, openness, intentionality, grace. Resilient leaders take action and respond. They design a stepby- step plan, look ahead, and focus on solutions (not the setbacks). We can all learn from them as role models for resilience.

THE LONELINESS OF LEADERSHIP

Schools are isolated, and leaders are even more so within the school. Patterson, Goens & Reed point out that pioneering leaders "act in isolation, are often criticized, mocked or ignored by the prevailing culture" (2009, p. 167). Loneliness is their human condition, and resilient leaders recognize the feeling and know that it is not permanent. In Margaret Wheatley's book *Perseverance* (2009), she admits that it is indeed lonely to get to the future first, and that leaders will always be a lonely, invisible minority. She reminds us that as our work deepens, and we find others to accompany us, we grow wiser, lower our expectations about what might be possible, and our emotional state becomes less compelling. We pay less attention to how we feel and just plain do the work! Indeed, leaders can feel abandoned, ignored, maligned, and unloved. However, these feelings pass through us if we let them. Wheatley says that loneliness eventually transforms itself into a willingness to be alone. However, we first have to let loneliness sit there, wait for it to pass through, and then notice that it is gone. We can survive and trust ourselves in the process (p. 85).

Another way to address loneliness is to give ourselves permission to be the vulnerable people who we already are. We can get ret rid of the "I can handle it, I don't need any help" mentality and reach out to colleagues who have been there, who have lived through a similar experience. Find your safety net and build a network of confidential, non-judgmental, listening ears who give honest feedback and support.

NURTURING OUR EMOTIONAL WELLBEING

There is a real reason why adults on the airplane are told to put the oxygen mask over their face first, before they put one on the face of a child. If we can't breathe, we can't be of any help to anyone else. It is essential that every instructional leader is getting the oxygen (in this case, emotional wellbeing) they need, so that they can lead everyone else. Expert on emotional intelligence Daniel Goleman calls this selfmanagement. Howard Gardner, the author of the theory of "multiple intelligences" calls this self-monitoring skill "intrapersonal intelligence". It means being attuned to our inner self to make sure that we are in a state of inner balance and harmony. Resilient leaders schedule dinner with friends, make sure they take a walk around the block, go to the gym, or when worse comes to worse, do the five minutes of deep breathing in the car before walking into the school to get some grounding, perspective, and inner balance.

Shonda Rhimes, the famed television hit show creator, talks about how she became so unbalanced that she spun out of control in a multitude of ways. What brought her back was a daughter who reminded her that it was "time to play". And so they played with her dolls, had pretend tea parties, and it was the art of mindless play that brought her back to a sense of priorities and focus that was lost in the stress and weight of both demands and success (*Year of Yes: How to Dance It Out, Stand in the Sun and Be Your Own Person*, 2015). Margaret Wheatley calls this "groundedness". We create groundedness by nurturing our convictions, learning from our experiences, and developing trust in ourselves and our world. We can't let attention on this lapse or we lose that inner balance. We can't assume that we automatically stay grounded. It is a learned skill of reflection, checking in with ourselves, and stepping out of ourselves periodically to take a temperature check of our wellbeing (*Perseverance*, 2009, p. 135). Wheatley also quotes a 14th-century samurai warrior to make a point (p. 134):

I have no parents: I make the heavens and earth my parents.

I have no home: I make awareness my home.

I have no divine power: I make honesty my divine power.

I have no means: I make understanding my means.

I have no magic secrets: I make character my magic secret.

I have no miracles: I make right action my miracles.

I have no friends: I make my mind my friend.

I have no enemy: I make carelessness my enemy.

I have no armor: I make benevolence and righteousness my armor.

THE ROLE OF SPIRITUALITY

Building our resilience means knowing that in challenging times we need to trust the universe and the support it provides. This concept is bigger than religion. It means trusting that there is a higher power. It reminds us that we are connected to each other and not alone. The universe gives us what we need. We need to know that, and we need to know how to ask for what we need. When the challenge is so overwhelming and our fear is so big, it is time to give it up to the universe, to the angels, and ask the spirit to give you strength, wisdom, and clarity. Spirituality reminds us to be grateful and to express gratitude at every chance we can. We are God's voice on this earth and are grateful to lean on his wisdom.

PRACTICE PERSEVERANCE

Rather than labeling yourself with what you have been through in your life (cancer survivor, divorcee, widow), name yourself for the future life you envision. Your vision of the future asks you to be fearless and brave. Perseverance isn't about aggression and bravado. Rather, it suggests that we model internalized, quiet strength Perseverance means that when we feel lost, we stop reaching for old maps and predictable responses. In *Leading with Soul* Bolman & Deal (2001) discuss the need to hone a counterintuitive response when we have lost our way. In fact, the worst thing to do is to follow a pre-designed map. We need to stop, breathe, and consider what we can learn from this new world. We need to open wide our eyes and look around. Take note of all the new information we can collect. Yes, we are lost. But in truth, we are not. We are right here. We will design new maps when we are calm, curious, and organized enough for what we need. We embrace perseverance by standing steadfast, clear and grounded in our beliefs. We remind ourselves that these situations are not about quick fixes but about hunkering down for a marathon run. The self-talk of marathon runners (pacing yourself, breathing differently and deeply, making sure you have supporters and cheerleaders at the 13th and 20th miles when you are ready to drop, drinking water along the way) apply for a leadership long run as well.

HOW ADAPTIVE ARE YOU?

Encyclopedia Britannica was at a crossroads. Their sales of the old, familiar 28-volume hardbound set of books were plummeting. If they clung to the idea that their identity was leather-bound to the books, they would be going out of business for sure. They had to dig deeply, reflect, and discuss, "Are we about the medium or are we about the mission?" After much soul searching, they decided that it was about their mission – to be the foremost facilitator and provider of knowledge. The format of how you access that knowledge was less important. So they voted to discontinue the book series and move their platform to online access only. Now they can update and include new information very quickly, as opposed to waiting for the next book revision. Their sales have increased. They have reinvented and reenergized themselves as a company. They modeled what being adaptive looks like. They proved that it is possible to adjust strategies without ever compromising values.

Resilient leaders are adaptive. They seek and use ongoing feedback to embrace modifications and adaptations. Their ego is not intertwined with the end result. They don't waste energy on mistakes. They use them as reflective opportunities to hone a skill, adapt, and move forward. Margaret Wheatley clarifies this when she says, "The leader's role is not to make sure that people know exactly what to do and when to do it. Instead, leaders need to ensure that there is strong and evolving clarity about who the organization is. When this clear identity is available, it serves every member of the organization. Even in chaotic circumstances, individuals can make congruent decisions. Turbulence will not cause the organization to dissolve into incoherence.

In this category, we need leaders. But we don't need bosses. We need leaders to help us develop the clear identity that likes the dark moments of confusion. We need leaders to support us as we learn how to live by our values. We need leaders who understand that we are best controlled by concepts that invite our participation, not policies and procedures that curtail our contribution." (Wheatley, 1999, p. 131)

Building Your Instructional Leadership

WHAT RESILIENT LEADERSHIP LOOKS LIKE?

1. Anticipate all of the ways your plan will be disrupted, disturbed, blown up... and plan for it. Practice not being surprised and pull out Plan B.

2. Use your positive influence to make something good happen.

3. Take the time to analyze the reality of external forces that could limit what you want to accomplish and strategically address them before they do.

4. Search for the positive aspects of adversity to balance the negative ones.

5. Privately clarify and publicly articulate in a consistent way your leadership core values (e.g., acting in a trustworthy way, demonstrating compassion for all people, making all decisions through the lens of what is best for the students).

6. Model confidence that we can learn from adversity and be better because of it.

7. Build your personal support base and use it in turbulent times. Don't hesitate to share doubts and fears with people you trust and ask for support.

8. Reread the "Serenity Prayer". Accept the things you cannot change and look forward to all that is working. Turn your face to the light.

9. Model and share gratitude for the strength that was given to all of us, for the team that supports each other, and for all of you individually who have faith.

10. Stay focused on the priorities and don't allow yourself to get sidetracked or worn down.

Chapter 15 / Building Your Own Resilience

STRATEGIES TO BUILD RESILIENCE

1. Take a self-care assessment[1] in the categories of physical, mental, emotional, practical, social, and spiritual and graph your results. What does your overall pattern look like? Which areas are strongest and which are weakest?

2. Create a realistic self-care intention statement for each of the categories above. Now do them in your real life and discuss the effect with your colleagues.

3. Apply for the job "facilitator of reflective practice" described below. Underline the action words, and reflect on how you embody them in your work.

   "A person who is inherently curious; someone who doesn't have all the answers and isn't afraid to admit it; someone who is confident enough in his or her ability to accept challenges in a non-defensive manner; someone who is secure enough to make his or her thinking public and therefore subject to discussion; someone who is a good listener; someone who likes other people and trusts them to make the right decisions if given the opportunity; someone who is able to see things from another's perspective and is sensitive to the needs and feelings of others; someone who is able to relax and lean back and let others assume the responsibility for their own learning. Some experience desirable but not as important as the ability to learn from mistakes." (Osterman and Kottkamp, 1993, p. 64)

4. Identify three core values that drive your decision making. Crosswalk them with your actions and analyze the correlation.

5. Write your resilience eulogy. What attributes do you want to highlight about yourself?

6. Identify your most favorite professional mistake because you learned a very important lesson from it. What was the mistake and what did you learn? What do you do differently now because of it?

7. Think of five things to be grateful for today.

8. Create a "one-a-day" wellbeing activity schedule and stick to it.

9. Collect feedback from your faculty or colleagues about something in your practice you are curious about. Analyze the data and make a change because of it.

10. Practice personal, professional, and spiritual mindfulness. Be still... if only for five minutes in your car in the parking lot before you walk in to the onslaught. Breathe in life and light. "Life, like muddy waters, becomes clear and calm after we stop throwing rocks and stirring up the dirt." Jen Moff

---

[1] available at: http://www.mediafire.com/view/27zv095kus97i07/Soul-Warriors.com_-_Self-Care_Assessment.pdf (page 3).

BIBLIOGRAPHY

Bolman, L. G., & Deal, T. E. (2001). *Leading with Soul: An Uncommon Journey of Spirit*. San Francisco, CA: Jossey-Bass.

Chödrön, P. (2001). *The Places That Scare You: A Guide to Fearlessness in Difficult Times*. Boston, MA: Shambala Publications.

Gardner, H. (2011). *Frames of Mind: The Theory of Multiple Intelligences* (3rd ed.). New York, NY: Basic Books.

Garmston, R., & B. Wellman (2013). *The Adaptive School: A Sourcebook for Collaborative Groups* (2nd ed.). Plymouth: Rowan and Littlefield Publishers.

Goleman, D. (1995). *Emotional Intelligence: Why It Can Matter More Than IQ*. New York, NY: Bantam Books.

Heifetz, R. A., Linsky, M., & Grashow, A. (2009). *The Practice of Adaptive Leadership: Tools and Tactics for Changing Your Organization and the World*. Cambridge, MA: Harvard Business Press.

Kidd, S. M. (2002). *The Secret Life of Bees*. New York, NY: Penguin Books.

Osterman, K., & Kottkamp, R. (1993). *Reflective practice for educators: Improving schooling through professional development*. Newbury Park, CA: Corwin Press

Patterson, J. L., & Kelleher, P. (2005). *Resilient School Leaders: Strategies for Turning Adversity into Achievement*. Alexandria, VA: Association for Supervision and Curriculum Development.

Patterson, J., Goens, G., & Reed D. (2009). *Resilient Leadership for Turbulent Times: A Guide to Thriving in the Face of Adversity*. New York, NY: Rowman & Littlefield Education.

Pink, D. H. (2012). *To Sell Is Human: The Surprising Truth About Moving Others*. New York, NY: Riverhead Books.

Rhimes, S. (2015). *Year of Yes: How to Dance It Out, Stand in the Sun and Be Your Own Person*. New York, NY: Simon & Schuster.

Seligman, M. E. P. (2006). *Learned Optimism: How to Change your Mind and Your Life*. New York, NY: Vintage Books.

Sogunro, O. A. (2012). *Stress in School Administration: Coping Tips for Principals*. Journal of School Leadership, (22)3, 664–700.

Wheatley, M. J. (1999). *Leadership and the New Science*. San Francisco, CA: Berrett-Koehler Publishers.

Wheatley, M. (2009). *Turning to One Another: Simple Conversations to Restore Hope in The Future*. San Francisco, CA: Berrett-Koehler Publishers.

Wheatley, M. (2010). *Perseverance*. San Francisco, CA: Berrett-Koehler Publishers.

Williamson, M. (1992). *A Return to Love: Reflections on the Principles of a Course in Miracles*. New York, NY: HarperCollins Publishing.

York-Barr, J. (2006). *Reflective Practice to Improve Schools: An Action Guide for Educators*. Thousand Oaks, CA: Corwin Press.

APPENDIX

Relational complexities:

Relationships are the foundation for instructional leadership. The concept of relationships includes the relationship you have with yourself as a leader, the relationships you foster between the members of your team, and the ones you establish with every adult group with whom you work. The groundwork for these relationships begins with building an environment of psychological safety. A safe environment invites you to reflect on how you build relationships through intentional empathy, how you model and facilitate an environment of trust for all of those around you, and how you create and support structures for collaboration through your school. Building trust among adults, creating a psychologically safe environment to learn and grow together, and skills for collaboration and team building are the focus of your leadership skillset for intentional relationship building.

Relational criteria	Mastery/ Distinguished	Proficient/ Competent/ Skilled	Aspiring	Novice
1. Creates a psychologically safe environment for faculty and students.	Intellectual risks are applauded and mistakes are embraced as learning opportunities; alternative viewpoints are sought and expected; posing questions and seeking feedback are consistently modeled and the collaborative norm.	Intellectual risks are often times applauded and mistakes are usually reframed as learning opportunities. Alternative viewpoints are often sought. Feedback is often sought. Inquiry and collaboration is frequently modeled.	Teachers are not sure whether alternative opinions and ideas are embraced. Occasional questions are solicited and appreciated. Feedback is occasionally sought. Mistakes are sometimes reframed and sometimes seen as negative. Teachers do not seek to surface real conversation with the leadership.	Fosters an environment where teachers are fearful about expressing opinions and ideas, and are not willing to ask questions. Mistakes are seen as negative and are dealt with punitively. Feedback is solicited or not appreciated by the leadership. Real conversation among the teachers takes place in the parking lot.

Appendix

Relational criteria	Mastery/ Distinguished	Proficient/ Competent/ Skilled	Aspiring	Novice
2. Cultivates empathy and compassion.	Models seeking to understand and taking the perspective of another; withholds judgment and practices active listening; recognizes emotion in other people and seeks to provide emotional support	With frequency, the leader seeks to understand the perspective of another; withholds judgment and practices active listening; often recognizes emotion in other people. Often seeks to provide emotional support	Occasionally seeks agendas other than his/her own. Occasionally seeks to collect informal or formal data from the faculty about their feelings, reactions or input into decision making. Occasionally judges and interrogates others in conversation.	Seeks to push his/her personal agenda consistently. Does not seek to collect informal or formal data from the faculty about their feelings, reactions or input into decision making. Consistently judges and interrogates others in conversation.
3. Builds highly functional, collaborative teams/ departments.	Creates an environment of trust, honest and respectful dialogue and discussion, accountability, the collaborative study of results and the collegial interchange among professionals	Supports the idea of the creation of an environment of trust, honest and respectful dialogue and discussion, accountability, the collaborative study of results and the collegial interchange among professionals	Occasionally attempts to address the concept of trust and the facilitation of dialogue and discussion. Respectful interaction happens inconsistently. Leader attempts to avoid giving mixed, incomplete or omitted messages. Team collaboration is encouraged inconsistently.	Facilitates a lack of trust, where dialogue is shut down, discussion is not invited and disrespect is modeled. Mixed, incomplete or omitted messages are fostered. Team collaboration is discouraged. Isolation is encouraged as a "divide and conquer" approach to leadership.
4. Facilitates a continuous learning environment	Models and expects intellectual inquiry and curiosity, promotes data driven feedback. Collaborative structures for adults to observe and learn from each other are embedded and consistent.	Often models and expects intellectual inquiry and curiosity, promotes data driven feedback, Periodically provides collaborative structures for adults to observe and learn from each other.	Inquiry about data of student progress is sometimes modeled or sought. Occasionally teachers participate in collaborative interaction or learning from each other.	Inquiry about data of student progress is not modeled or sought. Teachers do not participate in collaborative interaction or learning from each other.

Building Your Instructional Leadership

Instructional complexities:

Instructional leaders support a common language of expert instruction, as defined by the Teaching and Learning Framework which correlates with student achievement. The instructional leader expects to see clarifying learning targets and the criteria for success which support them in every classroom. The leader looks and asks teachers to be guided by evidence of student learning and proposes protocols for formative assessment of the collected evidence. The instructional leader discusses and models the skills and tools for providing descriptive feedback, and expects that teachers provide descriptive feedback to students which is aligned to the learning targets. The leader facilitates skill building among the faculty to that all instruction is culturally relevant and every classroom is a culturally safe environment.

Instructional leaders know how to observing classroom instruction and provide data-driven feedback. They address mediocre teaching, offer coaching conversations and design support structures to foster professional growth.

Instructional criteria	Mastery/ Distinguished	Proficient/ Competent/ Skilled	Aspiring	Novice
1. Provides clarity of instructional expectations in planning, teaching pedagogy, assessment and feedback	Diagnoses classroom instruction through the consistent alignment of learning targets, embedded formative assessments, descriptive feedback and modifying instruction based on evidence of student learning.	Often times diagnoses classroom instruction using alignment of learning targets, embedded formative assessments, descriptive feedback and modifying instruction based on evidence of student learning.	Occasionally spends time in classrooms to observe and collect data of best teaching practice. Occasional descriptive feedback is provided. Occasionally the connection between presence of learning targets, alignment of activities to learning targets, formative assessment in support of learning target mastery, and descriptive feedback in response to learning targets is documented and discussed with teachers.	Finds it difficult to manage and spend time in classrooms to observe and collect data of best teaching practice. If feedback is provided it is of a generic and general nature. The connection between presence of learning targets, alignment of activities to learning targets, formative assessment in support of learning target mastery, and descriptive feedback in response to learning targets is not documented or discussed with teachers.

©The Learning Collaborative

Instructional criteria	Mastery/ Distinguished	Proficient/ Competent/ Skilled	Aspiring	Novice
2. Provides instructional coaching support to teachers	Provides data driven feedback. Consistently poses coaching questions to deepen reflection and investigation of teaching methodology to increase student achievement	Often provides data driven feedback. Inconsistently poses coaching questions to deepen reflection and investigation of teaching methodology to increase student achievement	Occasionally provides advice and directs teachers on how to fix it. Occasionally shares opinions, rather than posing reflective questions. Periodically provides data to support opinions.	Tells teachers what he/she believes is wrong and provides advice on how to fix it. Consistently shares opinions, rather than posing reflective questions. Does not provide data to support opinions.
3. Addresses mediocre teaching	Diagnoses mediocrity with specificity and consistently provides appropriate supervisory response to each type of mediocrity (lack of content and planning expertise; limiting beliefs; impact of external influences)	Often diagnoses mediocrity with specificity and often provides appropriate supervisory response to each type of mediocrity (lack of content and planning expertise; limiting beliefs; impact of external influences)	Occasionally addresses mediocre teaching by pretending not to notice; Sometimes exhibits the courage to address it; occasionally exhibits motivation to address it with appropriate supporting data and communication skills.	Does not address mediocre teaching by pretending not to notice; being afraid to address it; being unmotivated to address it or not having the data and communication skills to address it.
4. Builds a "No Secrets" school through the collection of multiple data sources, data-driven dialogue and learning focused supervision	Fosters transparency of multiple sources of data on student progress with teachers; supports the planning of targeted next steps and scaffolded support for teachers to address student needs.	Often fosters transparency of multiple sources of data on student progress with teachers; inconsistently supports the planning of targeted next steps and scaffolded support for teachers to address student needs.	Occasionally teachers are provided with the reasons behind decisions being made; Occasionally expectations for teachers and students are shared or revisited; teachers receive occasional instructional support. Sometimes data-driven dialogue occurs.	Fosters a "Secret School" where reasons for decisions are not communicated; expectations for teachers and students are unknown; how and when teachers receive support is unknown. Data-driven dialogue is not present.

Situational Complexities:

Instructional leaders are always anticipating breakdowns (organizational and interpersonal) before they happen. They anticipate "initiative fatigue" and faculty boycotting change; they plan for difficult personalities adding toxin to the school atmosphere, and consistently work to preserve a healthy environment. They refuel their own resiliency before rock bottom hits.

Instructional leaders always seek to increase their disposition for strategic thinking and anticipation. Instructional leaders address complexities when facilitating professional growth for adults. They have courage and skills for having hard conversations, dealing with difficult people, and working with resistance and passive-aggressive behaviors.

Situational criteria	Mastery/ Distinguished	Proficient/ Competent/ Skilled	Aspiring	Novice
1. Anticipates difficult situations and their implications; has strategic responses thoughtfully planned.	Strategically thinks through all implications (students, parents, faculty, district office) before a complex decision is made; solicits input and thought partnership in thinking through decisions with multiple implications.	Often thinks strategically through all implications (students, parents, faculty, district office) before a complex decision is made; Usually solicits input and thought partnership in thinking through decisions with multiple implications.	Considers how decisions might be differentiated from simple to complex. Occasionally decisions are analyzed for implications and ramifications. Occasionally solicits input from a thought partner or leadership mentor to think through the situation together.	All decisions are treated the same-simple and complex. Decisions are made quickly and on the fly without thinking through implications and ramifications. Does not solicit input from a thought partner or leadership mentor to think through the situation together.
2. Models a repertoire of conferencing skills: coaching, collaborating, consulting, calibrating and courageous conferences.	Consistently communicates with faculty to address a variety of conference purposes, and consistently matches the conference skill and type with the appropriate context and teacher need.	Usually communicates with faculty to address a variety of conference purposes, and usually matches with accuracy the conference skill and type with the appropriate context and teacher need.	Attempts to expand his/her repertoire of conference strategies to address all personalities and contexts. Occasionally conference include data; discussion of next steps and two-way dialogue between the administrator to the teacher.	Provides one mode of conference to address all personalities and contexts. Conference does not include data; discussion of next steps and is one-sided from the administrator to the teacher.

Situational criteria	Mastery/ Distinguished	Proficient/ Competent/ Skilled	Aspiring	Novice
3. Supports faculty as they navigate through change	Consistently explains the reasons for the change; the process for the roll out of the change; the losses and gains to anticipate; the support and resources which will be offered as the change is navigated; and emotional support throughout the process	Usually explains the reasons for the change; the process for the roll out of the change; the losses and gains to anticipate; the support and resources which will be offered as the change is navigated; and emotional support throughout the process	Occasionally reasons for a change or initiative are shared with those needing to implement them. Sometimes provides emotional support to faculty when going through a change process. Occasionally provides support for learning new skills in a new context.	The reasons for any change and initiative are a secret to those needing to implement it. Emotional reaction to going through the process of change is dealt with punitively. Support for learning new skills in a new context is not provided.
4. Interacts appropriately with passive aggressive, aggressive and other difficult personalities	Consistently practices dispassionate data driven response to provocation; sabotage; negative and bullying behavior; proactively addresses and documents inappropriate behavior and clarifies expectations.	Often practices dispassionate data driven response to provocation; sabotage; negative and bullying behavior; proactively addresses and documents inappropriate behavior and clarifies expectations.	Occasionally utilizes skills to address passive aggressive behavior. Sometimes avoids power struggles and confrontations with aggressive personalities. Frequently becomes emotionally involved in all responses and takes personally what difficult people say in anger.	Does not notice or identify passive aggressive behavior. Builds power struggles and confrontations with aggressive personalities. Becomes emotionally involved in all responses, and take personally what difficult personalities say in anger.

ACKNOWLEDGMENTS

The famed poet Maya Angelou sung about "standing on the shoulders of giants" and that those giants were a part of her, holding her up every day of her life. I would like to acknowledge the giants who have been a part of my life, on whose shoulders I am so privileged to be standing.

I stand on the shoulders of William Brodsky, my 90-year-old father, who was an educator for 40 years. He was the informal dean of the principals for the School District of Philadelphia until he became the Director of Administrative Training for the city. Everyone knew that if you had an underperforming school, Bill Brodsky would turn it into a high performing one. Every aspiring leader knew that you needed to log time with Bill if you ever wanted to pass the required principal's exam. Every Saturday as a child, I found my father sitting around our dining room table tutoring his disciples, paid by his passion and giving forward to the profession he loved so much. I am a very grateful daughter.

I stand on the shoulders of my mother, Dr. Audrey Brodsky, a 40-year veteran educator and Pennsylvania State Teacher of the Year. I am the only person I know who has had a 40-year student teaching experience by virtue of being Audrey's daughter. We were a household of lesson plans, high expectations, intellectual power coupled with exhaustion, and a passion for learning.

I stand on the shoulders of my most gifted mentors:

- Dr. William Fitzpatrick, my first principal, who took a chance, hired me when I was 19, and made sure I earned a master's degree in administration immediately

- Dr. Dorothy Moore, Professor Emeritus at The George Washington University, who was my undergraduate and doctoral advisor and colleague when I taught university courses at GWU

- Dr. Robert "Bud" Spillane, Superintendent of Fairfax County Public Schools (FCPS) and Regional Program Officer for the U.S. Department of State, who opened that first door to the literal world of international schools for me and gave me the longest leave of absence in the history of FCPS, so I could test the waters of national and international consultancy

- Dr. Dolores Bohen, FCPS Assistant Superintendent for Communications and published author, who inherited a 24-year old green and brash version of myself to oversee 40 schools in support of their programs for the gifted. She taught me how to write, think strategically, design proposals, create systemic programs and be discreet

- Ms. Ann Jaekle, the FCPS principal that modeled every chapter in this book, reframing conflict, building teams and collaboration decades before her time.

I pull from the lessons from these giants every single day of my professional life.

Acknowledgments

I thank my thought partners and friends from whom I have learned so much: Heidi Hayes Jacobs, Bena Kallick, Mort Sherman, Jay McTighe, Carolyn McKanders, Jerry Newberry, and GJ Tarazi. I am humbled by their thinking, generosity of heart, mind, and spirit.

I stand on the shoulders of some beloved colleagues from Research for Better Teaching, when the incubation of great thinking began in a barn with Jon Saphier, Mary Ann Haley, Caroline Tripp, Andy Platt, and Deb Reed. That era brought a passion for collaboration and building capacity to life and a round table of opportunities to fruition. I am grateful to Sue McGregor and Judy Duffield in the second RBT phase, and the Montgomery County Public Schools Center for Skillful Leading and Teaching trainers for their great thinking and friendship. Our pursuit of other people who think around the same topics with passion lives on to this day.

I thank my international colleagues and friends who push my thinking and inspire me with their vision and great talent: Kathy Stetson, Executive Director of the Central and Eastern European Schools Association (CEESA), Emily Sargent-Beasley, Deputy Head of Shanghai American School, Michelle Kuhns, Director of Professional Learning at the American School of Dubai, Chip Barder, Director, and Megan Brazil, Elementary Principal, both at the United Nations International School in Hanoi, Viet Nam, the teachers and administrators of the Walworth Barbour American International School in Israel, and Dr. Robert Brindley, Director of the American International School of Bucharest, Romania.

I am grateful to stand shoulder to shoulder with champions in school systems around the United States who model exceptional instructional leadership every day: Dr. Aaron Spence, Superintendent, Rashard Wright, Chief Schools Officer, and our brother Kevin Hobbs—may he rest in peace—of Virginia Beach City Public Schools, Debbie Piper, Coordinator of Teacher Development and PAR Program Supervisor Jennifer Dunkle of Baltimore County Public Schools, Dr. Greg Hutchings, Superintendent at Shaker Heights and Dr. Talisa Dixon, Superintendent in Cleveland Heights, Ohio, Ms. Andrea Kane, Associate Superintendent for Academic Services in Richmond Public Schools, Andrea Zamora, Director of Professional Growth and Development and Zipporah Miller, Senior Manager of Organizational Learning for Anne Arundel County Public Schools. These colleagues are brilliant thinkers and leaders, passionate, kind, and never losing their sense of humor.

I stand on the shoulders of my family of choice, surrogate parents Arie and Shoshana Shoval, and surrogate brother Jerry Newberry, who have been my inspiration and support for the last 32 years.

Lastly, I thank my gifted editor Dado Čakalo, whose honesty, clarity, and attention to detail awe me with every review. I am so grateful to Ivan Mikulić and NoStressMarketing, whose graphic artistry, positive outlook and "Yes we can" mantra move mountains. I thank Miecha Galbraith, whose facilitation of book organizing and printing logistics has been invaluable. I am so lucky to work with the three of you.

Thank you so much.

ABOUT THE AUTHOR

Dr. Fran Prolman is the founder, president, and senior consultant of The Learning Collaborative, an internationally recognized teacher, administrator, author, consultant, and keynote speaker. She is known for her depth of knowledge, dynamism, energy, practical application, and proven track record of results.

Fran earned her doctorate in Teacher Training, International Education, and Organizational Development from George Washington University and a master's degree in Educational Administration and Curriculum and Instruction from the University of Pennsylvania. She has been a two-time Fulbright Scholar in India and Israel and has presented numerous papers, workshops, and keynote speeches nationally and internationally.

Fran brings more than 30 years of experience providing multifaceted work with organizations and school systems throughout the United States and the world. She was a member of the first Understanding by Design trainer cadre for the Association for Supervision and Curriculum Development (ASCD), designing curriculum training throughout the United States, a faculty member for ASCD, and a senior consultant at Research for Better Teaching, training trainers and educating thousands of administrators and teachers in effective learning practice. Fran focuses on building human capacity through a variety of avenues. She facilitates leadership retreats for teachers, administrators, and executives; delivers organization-wide keynote speeches and workshops, coaches to build highly functional teams; assists organizations and teams in the appropriate use of data, designs professional growth and evaluation systems, and brings insight to the change process.

She is a frequent presenter for the US Department of State, European Council of International Schools, the Association for Supervision and Curriculum Development, Central and Eastern European Schools Association, Near East South Asia Association of International Schools, African Association of International Schools, the Tri-Association for the Caribbean and Central America, and numerous client school systems in the United States.